SAXON MATH™

English Learners Handbook

SAXON™

A Harcourt Achieve Imprint

www.SaxonPublishers.com
1-800-284-7019

ISBN-13: 978-1-6003-2448-2

ISBN-10:   1-6003-2448-7

Printed in the United States of America

 6 7 8 9   028   14 13 12 11 10 09 08

TABLE OF CONTENTS

How *Saxon Math* Supports English Learners

For Students

Saxon Math provides English learners with the learning environment and approaches they need to acquire mathematical understanding and to learn mathematics effectively—right along with the rest of the student population. *Saxon Math* provides:

- A consistent lesson format that includes structured and predictable routines

- Multiple exposure to a concept through integrated and distributed instruction, practice, and review that always incorporate correct mathematical explanations and language

- Numerous opportunities for engaging in meaningful mathematical conversations—students hear, see, and use the language leading to an internalized understanding

- Visuals and pictures to show multiple representations of the concepts being taught

- Hands-on activities and concrete models to support conceptual learning

- An uncluttered textbook design using pictures only when they contribute directly to the content, enabling all students to concentrate on and be successful in mathematics

- Frequent and strategically placed formative and summative assessments, always cumulative in nature to gauge progress and monitor conceptual development and retention of skills

For Teachers

Saxon Math provides teachers with an approach that is effective for helping English learner students achieve maximum yearly progress. Research-based strategies for English learners are built into the daily lesson format.

- Teacher's Editions model the use of mathematical language daily to give students the academic language they need for success in mathematics courses and on standardized tests.

- The transcript for each lesson models for every teacher meaningful conversations about math. Students are ensured consistent presentation of content and development of mathematical language from teacher-to-teacher and school-to-school—and the right questions are asked to promote and develop higher-order thinking.

- English learners need hands-on activities to develop a deeper understanding of mathematical concepts. Lesson concepts and skills in *Saxon Math* are developed through engaging, hands-on/minds-on activities and rich mathematical conversations that are modeled and scripted for every teacher, and thus, *doable* by all teachers.

Additional English Learner Support

Saxon Math provides effective point-of-use strategies for English learners that focus on language acquisition, not on reteaching or simplifying the mathematics. These suggestions incorporate a four-step approach.

1. Define the word: students <u>hear</u> the word

2. Model the meaning of the word: students <u>see</u> and <u>connect</u> the word to its meaning

3. Check for understanding: students <u>talk</u> about and <u>explain</u> the meaning of the word

4. Apply in context: students <u>use</u> the word

For Spanish speakers, the Glossary within the *Saxon Math* program provides a Spanish translation of each vocabulary term and its definition.

This *English Learners Handbook* contains a wealth and variety of information that can be immediately used in the classroom. See the Table of Contents for focused support with a variety of languages that teachers may encounter in their mathematics classroom.

For students who are taught mathematics using Spanish, the complete *Saxon Matemáticas* is also available.

Student Language and Literacy Survey

Student Name: _____ **Date:** _____

The following surveys will provide insight into English language learners' language use and literacy practices in both their first languages and English. The surveys should be administered orally to each student in English or, if necessary, in the student's first language. If the person administering the surveys does not speak the student's first language, then paraprofessionals or bilingual students might be helpful in obtaining this information. The results of the surveys can be used to place each student in an appropriate program for English language learners and to inform instruction. Photocopy this page to document the information for each student.

HOME LANGUAGE SURVEY

Do you speak any other languages when you are not at school?   YES   NO
What languages? _____
How many years have you attended school in the U.S.? _____ years
How many years have you attended school in another country? _____ years

ORAL LANGUAGE SURVEY

Where do you speak _____ ?
(student's first language)

In school?	YES NO
At home?	YES NO
At the store?	YES NO
At the doctor's office?	YES NO
At restaurants or fast food places?	YES NO
Anywhere else? _____	

Where do you speak English?

In school?	YES NO
At home?	YES NO
At the store?	YES NO
At the doctor's office?	YES NO
At restaurants or fast food places?	YES NO
Anywhere else? _____	

LITERACY SURVEY

What do you read in _____ ?
(student's first language)

Magazines?	YES NO
Books?	YES NO
Mail?	YES NO
Information from the Internet?	YES NO
E-mails?	YES NO
Anything else? _____	

What do you read in English?

Magazines?	YES NO
Books?	YES NO
Mail?	YES NO
Information from the Internet?	YES NO
E-mails?	YES NO
Anything else? _____	

What do you write in _____ ?
(student's first language)

Letters?	YES NO
Notes?	YES NO
Information on forms?	YES NO
E-mails?	YES NO
Stories?	YES NO
Anything else? _____	

What do you write in English?

Letters?	YES NO
Notes?	YES NO
Information on forms?	YES NO
E-mails?	YES NO
Stories?	YES NO
Anything else? _____	

Developing Students' Oral Language

What Does It Mean to Know a Language?

Learning a new language is a complex undertaking. Children must learn English grammar, sounds, word forms, and word meanings (syntax, phonology, morphology, and semantics). They must be able to use the language to communicate in social situations and also to perform demanding academic functions in all content areas as well. They need to understand the kind of language appropriate to a variety of settings and the conventions which regulate communicating effectively within these settings. For academic success, children must be proficient in all four language processes—reading, writing, speaking, and listening *(Peregoy and Boyle 2001; Freeman and Freeman 2001)*.

It is important to distinguish between two fundamentally different types of language proficiency. Conversational language, sometimes referred to as **Basic Interpersonal Communication Skills (BICS)**, is social language—often called playground language. It is the language used in making friends, meeting basic needs, and comprehending everyday conversation. BICS is developed relatively rapidly and naturally, much as a child acquires his or her first language, through interaction with native speakers and input that is understandable to the child because of physical and visual context. Conversational language is well supported by context and is not cognitively demanding. BICS takes about two years to develop *(Cummins 2000)*.

Academic language, or **Cognitive Academic Language Proficiency (CALP)**, is the type of language necessary for success in school; it is the language of books, math, science, and social studies. It is more complex and abstract, with fewer concrete or visual clues to support meaning. Therefore, academic language typically is not well supported by context and is cognitively demanding. CALP is associated with higher-order thinking skills and is only achieved over time through meaningful language, literacy, and content instruction at children's appropriate Stages of Language Acquisition *(Cummins 2000)*. Academic language proficiency takes between five and seven years to develop.

English language learners do not need to develop CALP before content area learning is introduced. Rather, it is integrated language and content instruction that facilitates the simultaneous acquisition of academic language and academic content *(Samway and McKeon 1999)*. English language learners cannot afford to delay important learning in literacy, math, social studies, and science while they wait to acquire BICS first. Teachers need to provide instruction that addresses all language learners' needs simultaneously so that they can close the achievement gap between themselves and their native-speaking peers.

The Role of Family Members

It is clear from research that the academic and linguistic growth of children is enhanced when collaborative relationships are established between families and school *(Cummins 2000)*. Children who read to family members make significantly greater progress in literacy and English language development, even when their parents are neither fluent speakers of English nor literate. Children whose families are involved in their learning show greater interest in learning and behave better in school than those whose families are not involved.

Family involvement in their children's formal education has often been limited to attendance at open houses and report card conferences. Particularly in low-income schools, parents may come from backgrounds of little or no formal education themselves. School may be intimidating for these individuals and might conjure up negative emotions and experiences. These parents may feel inadequate in dealing with school personnel. Also, the relationship between teachers and parents in their home culture might discourage direct parental involvement *(Valdes 1996; Wong-Fillmore 1990)*. Sometimes this gives the mistaken impression that these parents do not care about their children or are not interested in their academic progress. Schools need to explore ways to encourage these parents to become involved in all aspects of their children's education.

Family involvement is more likely when families see the school and classroom as a **welcoming environment**. The presence of school staff or volunteers who speak their home language will facilitate family involvement. If asked, parents will often bring a trusted friend or family member who can serve as translator to conferences or meetings at school. This puts parents at ease and solves a problem for the staff members who do not speak the parents' language.

Families of English language learners should be regarded as a **valuable resource** for their own children and for others in school. They need to be empowered to share in policy- and decision-making about their children and the educational community in general. When schools and families work together, students succeed and communities are strengthened.

The Role of Culture

Acquiring a language involves more than simply speaking, reading, and writing the language. It involves thought patterns, perceptions, cultural values, communication styles, and social organizations.

A child's culture operates as a lens through which he or she views the world. Often the culture and language use in the classroom may conflict with what the child has learned in the home culture and language. Sometimes these differences may interfere with learning or participation in activities. Test performance, group interactions, responses to questioning, homework practices, and learning styles may all be ways in which the culture of the home conflicts with the culture of the classroom. Awareness of these differences will help you deal with them effectively. As children learn English, their success depends on their ability to adapt to the culture of the community. Teachers can facilitate this acculturation process by bridging the culture and language gap for their children. A variety of routines and approaches can help to increase comfort and success in your classroom. These include valuing the contributions of home languages and cultures, allowing the use of the home language in the classroom when appropriate, encouraging children to make connections to their past experiences and contribute their viewpoints, fostering family involvement in the classroom and in school, and pursuing specific information about the cultures of the children and their families.

Some Myths and Misconceptions about Language Acquisition

There are a number of myths and misconceptions commonly held in today's society regarding second language acquisition. We hope the research-based facts presented here will help you dispel these myths.

Myth: **English language learners simply need to be placed in an English learning environment, and they'll pick up English naturally in one year.**
Fact: While this approach works well for the acquisition of social English, the acquisition of academic English requires skillful instruction that reaches the child with a limited command of English. Children who receive little or no instruction tailored to the needs of language learners can take as many as ten years to achieve grade level performance in the content areas (Collier 1995).

Myth: If children can already speak English, they don't need any further specialized instruction.

Fact: Even though English language learners may give the impression of being able to speak English well on the playground or with their peers, we know that it typically takes five to seven years for them to acquire grade-level competence in academic subject areas. Integrated instruction in language, literacy, and content can help children acquire academic skills as they learn language. Effective instruction can help reduce this academic gap (Collier 1995).

Myth: Transfer occurs automatically from the primary language to English.

Fact: Although it is known that some transfer between languages does occur naturally, we can organize our instruction to maximize the transfer of learning. Similarities between the two languages should be explicitly pointed out in instruction so that children develop metalinguistic awareness and the ability to analyze language patterns. With this in mind, we should also recognize that the higher the level of development of the child's primary language, the better his or her chances at success in the second language will be. Therefore, we should encourage parents to maintain the home language and continue to foster its development in their children (Cummins 2000).

Myth: English language learners should not be exposed to English print until they are orally proficient in English.

Fact: Although this belief was held widely in the past, we now know that second language acquisition is aided by exposure to literacy. We can and should begin literacy instruction right from the start. Although written language seems to rely upon oral language, there are strategies for developing language and literacy simultaneously. Exposure to print helps children build visual literacy and remember what they have learned. Introducing literacy at the outset of English acquisition allows children to progress most rapidly toward academic success (Freeman and Freeman 2000).

Myth: Children need to become proficient readers in their native language before learning to read in their second language.

Fact: While research supports the importance of primary language reading in overall literacy development, current research shows that literacy can proceed simultaneously in two languages, and that there is no reason to delay second language literacy. Reading skills acquired in one language can transfer to the other and vice versa (Cummins 2000).

English Learners in the Mathematics Classroom

Instruction in mathematics to English learners should not be "watered down." Students often are capable of **higher-order thinking skills** but just lack the knowledge of English and the knowledge of the language of mathematics in English to communicate their ideas. *(See the section in this book on Mathematics Instruction in Other Countries.)* Encourage students to analyze, justify, represent and use other higher-order thinking skills within the various methods of communication described below.

Techniques for Aiding Instruction

English language learners need to be able to use English to communicate in social settings and to achieve academically in all content areas, including mathematics. For this to happen, teachers must provide comprehensible input—language that is understandable to language learners because it is contextualized and meaningful—in both oral and written English. Instruction in the language-learning classroom should be supported by strategies such as gesturing, restating, and acting out—strategies that enhance and support meaning. In this way, instruction becomes meaningful (in other words, the input becomes comprehensible) to children whose command of English is limited.

Teachers can make instruction comprehensible to children by using the following techniques:

Verbal

- Paraphrasing, or saying the same thing in different ways

- Using frequent repetition and restatement

- Keeping oral explanations short and simple

- Varying speech volume to emphasize key vocabulary

- Pausing during discussions to provide time for students to respond

Non-verbal

- Employing gestures, movements, and other body language to emphasize meaning

- Using Total Physical Response, a technique in which children respond physically to commands given orally by the teacher or another child

Scaffolded Instruction

- Previewing and reviewing lessons (in children's primary languages, whenever possible)

- Introducing new math vocabulary at the beginning of the lesson and reviewing previously-taught math terms that will be used in the day's lesson

- Instructing in small increments and using step-by-step teaching to give children time to process what they are learning in mathematics

- Modeling and demonstrating, in addition to verbally describing, math concepts and procedures to increase understanding

- Including guided practice in order to demonstrate and discuss math problems, while monitoring student understanding

- Connecting to children's prior knowledge and educational experiences, as well as to other subject areas the child is studying

- Checking frequently for understanding and providing feedback

Models, Charts, and Visuals

- Using math manipulatives or concrete models to demonstrate concepts

- Using visuals, diagrams, real-world objects, and audiovisual aids as examples of concepts and vocabulary

- Using graphic organizers, semantic webs, and charts to show the relationships between ideas

- Writing key words and ideas on the board or easel pad so that language input is slowed down and children can remember it

Student Interaction

- Placing students in small groups or pairs and asking them to explain concepts and vocabulary to one another or to work the math problems together

- Providing hands-on activities for children to explore and demonstrate math concepts using manipulatives or other common objects

- Using children as linguistic and cultural resources by allowing them to explain vocabulary in their language or describe word-problem contexts from their culture

- Encouraging children to show they understand with gestures, movements, or short answers

- Using Language Experience Approach (LEA), a technique in which children dictate words, phrases, or sentences about a shared experience to the teacher

Our first job as teachers of English language learners is to provide **comprehensible input**. Children often go through a silent period. Once they do start to talk, however, we need to respond to their message rather than correcting what they say. At the same time, we can **model correct language** as we interact with English learners. If we constantly correct children, they may become afraid to use their developing English. When asked *Go bathroom?*, the teacher can model the correct language in his or her response without interrupting the purpose of the conversation: *You need to go to the bathroom? Sure, you may do that.*

Similarly, the classroom atmosphere should be one that is inviting and comfortable for language learners. If children are nervous or bored, it is as if a filter goes up and blocks them from learning language. On the other hand, if children are motivated and interested, the filter goes down, allowing language acquisition to take place. This is known as lowering the *affective filter*. We as teachers need to create a low-anxiety environment in which children feel comfortable taking language-learning risks. Rather than calling on children individually and using traditional tests that may raise the affective filter, we need to engage them in collaborative activities, encourage volunteering, validate attempts to produce language, and use a variety of ways to assess performance.

Children need a **comfortable, supportive environment** for learning in which they feel confident in taking risks with the new language, are given adequate time for developing **higher-order thinking skills and academic language**, and receive instruction that fulfills their needs in language, literacy, and content learning. Activities should be appropriate for children at a variety of Levels of Language Acquisition, with the teacher skillfully modifying whole-class instruction for groups of children with varying English proficiencies. Children need to be invited to use all of their senses in hands-on, meaningful activities instead of hearing an endless, incomprehensible stream of speech.

The chart on the following page summarizes the characteristics of a mathematics classroom environment that is supportive to English learning.

Characteristics of Classrooms that Support Language Learning

Low affective filter	The classroom atmosphere is encouraging and makes students feel comfortable and willing to participate and take risks.
Comprehensible input	Supportive strategies make math concepts and vocabulary understandable to students at the various levels of language acquisition.
Focus on communication	Language is real and is used for authentic, meaningful purposes rather than merely for its own sake.
Contextualized language	Context, visuals, examples, models, and diagrams provide support for oral language interaction and mathematics instruction.
Error acceptance	The message, rather than linguistic correctness, is the focus. Errors in English usage are corrected through teacher modeling of correct forms.
Increased wait time	Adequate time for formulating responses aids in second language production.
Respect for Levels of Language Acquisition	Activities chosen are developmentally appropriate for a variety of levels of language acquisition. Language instruction allows learners to stretch their skills and progress to higher levels.
Student-centered activities	Small group and partner activities provide authentic contexts for communication and language use. Student participation and interaction is encouraged.
Use of first language and home culture	When students are allowed to process information with each other in their first language, they maintain self-esteem, build a sense of community, and are able to transfer learning form one language to another. When home culture is used as an asset to classroom instruction, avenues to student participation are opened.
Authentic assessment based on multiple measures	Multiple measures, including oral assessments, daily observations, observational checklists, written assessments, student explanations, rubrics, and student work samples—when embedded in instruction—provide the teacher with appropriate information for use in planning further instruction.

Mathematics Instruction in Other Countries

Many English learners bring mathematics knowledge with them. However, they may have been taught different symbols or algorithms in their country of origin. While students understand the mathematics, they may exhibit confusion or uncertainty with the processes being taught in U.S. classrooms. By understanding these variations, teachers will be able to help English learners bridge the differences in terminology and procedures and thus become even more successful in mathematics.

A positive teaching moment might be to demonstrate to the whole class the algorithms used in other countries. This will not only make English learners more comfortable in the classroom and validate their prior learning but will also provide English speakers with additional methods of solution.

Math Language Issues

LARGE NUMBER PLACE VALUE. In some countries, spaces are used to indicate place value, instead of the commas used in the U.S. For example: 5,450,000 might be written as 5 450 000.

U.S. CUSTOMARY SYSTEM. Most of the world uses the metric system, with all measurements converted using a power of 10.

$$1 \text{ meter} = 100 \text{ centimeters}; 1 \text{ centimeter} = 10 \text{ millimeters}$$

Most students will not be familiar with the U.S. Customary System measurements (e.g., inches, quarts) and may become confused by the inconsistent conversion factor between units.

$$1 \text{ yard} = 3 \text{ feet}; 1 \text{ foot} = 12 \text{ inches}$$

ENGLISH HOMONYMS. Words that sound the same but have different meanings may be problematic for English learners. Consider the words *sum* and *some,* or the words *write* and *right.* Many of these words are used in mathematics instruction so special care should be taken when using them in explanations.

WORDS WITH MULTIPLE MEANINGS. English learners often have trouble with a word that can have different meanings depending on the context. It is important to point out which meaning you are using when the word appears in a discussion. Here is one example of just some of the definitions of a commonly-used English word, which also has an additional precise mathematical definition.

WORD	DEFINITION	USAGE
Right	opposite of left; east when facing north	"Raise your right hand."
Right	correct, accurate	"You're right."
Right	entitlement, freedom	"It's my right. I have the right to do that."
Right	well, healthy	"I don't feel right today."
Right	straight, without deviating	"I went right to work on my homework."
Right	90 degrees	"a right angle"

WORDS WITH MATHEMATICAL DEFINITIONS. Mathematics vocabulary terms often have common English definitions. Because these words may be used by English learners in conversational English, students may become confused when trying to learn the specific mathematical definition.

WORD	COMMON DEFINITION	MATH DEFINITION
Obtuse	Slow to understand	Between 90 degrees and 180 degrees
Plane	An airplane; a vehicle with wings and an engine that is heavier than air but is able to fly	A flat surface that extends without end in all directions
Power	Authority, strength	A number that can be expressed using an exponent
Rational	Reasonable, sensible, logical	A number that can be expressed as the ratio of two integers, with the denominator not 0
Table	A piece of furniture with a flat top and one or more legs	A chart with rows and columns to record data
Yard	The land surrounding a house	A length equal to 3 feet or 36 inches

Math Algorithms from Other Countries

English learners may understand mathematical operations but may have been taught different algorithms for subtraction, multiplication, and division. Some of these processes rely more on mental computation so students may not be used to writing down all the steps. Teachers should understand that students do comprehend these operations but just have a different background experience. The following examples will help teachers when confronted with English learners who provide alternative solutions to arithmetic problems.

Subtraction

Students in the U.S. learn to subtract by "borrowing" or decomposition of the minuend.

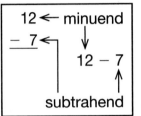

Equal Additions Method

Students in other countries learn the "equal additions" method. The same number is added to both the minuend and the subtrahend, which does not change the result. This allows students to either use mental math or subtract more easily.

$$\begin{array}{r} 46 + 1 \\ -29 + 1 \\ \hline \end{array} \qquad \begin{array}{r} 47 \\ -30 \\ \hline 17 \end{array}$$

Add 1 to the subtrahend to get a rounded number.
At the same time, add 1 to the minuend.
1 has been added to both numbers. Subtract to get 17.

$$\begin{array}{r} 32 \\ -17 \\ \hline \end{array} \qquad \begin{array}{r} 3\,{}^1 2 \\ -{}_2 1\,7 \\ \hline 1\,5 \end{array}$$

Add 10 ones to the 2 in the minuend to get 12 ones.
At the same time, add 10 to the 10 in the subtrahend to get 20.
10 has been added to both numbers. Subtract to get 15.

This process can be used for three-digit numbers and above by just repeating the equal additions to the next successive place values.

$$\begin{array}{r} 534 \\ -256 \\ \hline \end{array} \qquad \begin{array}{r} 5\,3\,{}^1 4 \\ -2\,{}^6 5\,6 \\ \hline 8 \end{array}$$

Add 10 ones to the minuend to get 14.
At the same time, add 10 to the subtrahend to get 60.
10 has been added to both numbers.
Subtract to get 8 in the ones place.

$$\begin{array}{r} 534 \\ -256 \\ \hline \end{array} \qquad \begin{array}{r} 5\,{}^1 3\,{}^1 4 \\ -{}_3 2\,{}^6 5\,6 \\ \hline 2\,7\,8 \end{array}$$

Add 10 tens to the minuend to get 13 tens.
At the same time, add 100 to the subtrahend to get 300.
100 has been added to both numbers.
Subtract the tens to get 7 in the tens place.
Subtract the hundreds to get 2 in the hundreds place.

Multiplication

Students in the U.S. learn to multiply by "carrying" during vertical multiplication problems.

Using the Distributive Property

Students in other countries use both the distributive property and the associative property to write out their steps to vertical multiplication.

15	$10 + 5$	Think of 15 as 10 + 5.
$\times 34$	$\times 30 + 4$	Think of 34 as 30 + 4.
20		Multiply 4 by 5.
40		Multiply 4 by 10.
150		Multiply 30 by 5.
300		Multiply 30 by 10.
510		Add to get the product.

Division

Students in the U.S. learn to divide by using long division with the $\overline{)}$ symbol.

$6 \div 2$

$2\overline{)6}$ ← dividend
↑
divisor

Using Mental Math

Students in other countries use several different methods, but most compute some of the steps mentally. So there will be fewer steps written on English learners' papers.

Method 1: Divide 204 by 6.

This method uses a similar format as the U.S. approach but includes more mental math steps.

$6 \div 2$

$2\overline{)6}$ ← dividend
↑
divisor

$6\overline{)204}$ — Think of this problem as 204 divided into 6 equal groups.

$6\overline{)204}$ with quotient 3, remainder 2 — First, think of 20 tens divided by 6. There are 3 groups of 6. Write the 3 in the quotient's place. Since $3 \times 6 = 18$, there is a remainder of 2 when $20 - 18$. Write the 2 under the 20.

$6\overline{)204}$ with quotient 34, 24, 0 — Bring down the 4 to get 24. Divide 24 by 6. There are 4 groups of 6 in 24. Write the 4 in the quotient's place. Since $4 \times 6 = 24$, there is a remainder of 0. Write the 0 under the 24.

$204 \div 6 = 34$

Method 2: Divide 204 by 6.

This method uses a different format from the U.S. approach, with the division numbers in the same order as in the problem. It also includes more mental math steps.

$$6 \div 2$$

$$6 \underline{\lfloor 2} \longleftarrow \text{divisor}$$
$$\uparrow$$
dividend

204 $\underline{\lfloor 6}$
  2   3

Divide 20 tens by 6. You get 3 because $3 \times 6 = 18$.
Write the 3 in the quotient's place.
The remainder is 2 when you subtract $20 - 18$.
Write the 2 under the 20.

204 $\underline{\lfloor 6}$
 24 34
  0

Bring down the 4 to get 24.
Divide 24 by 6. You get 4 because $4 \times 6 = 24$.
Write the 4 in the quotient's place.
The remainder is 0 when you subtract $24 - 24$.
Write the 0 under the 24.

$$204 \div 6 = 34$$

Mathematics Vocabulary in Nine Languages

ENGLISH	ARABIC	CHINESE SIMPLIFIED	CHINESE TRADITIONAL	HMONG
A				
above	أعلى	在上面；在…之上；超过，高过	在上面；在…之上；超過，高過	saum toj
acute angle	زاوية حادة	锐角	銳角	lub ces kaum me dua 90 feem pua
acute triangle	مثلث حاد الزوايا	锐角三角形	銳角三角形	lub muaj peb lub ces kaum uas me dua 90 feem pua
add	يجمع	加	加	sib ntxiv
addend	الكمية المضافة	加数	加數	cov zauv los sib ntxiv
addition	جمع	加法	加法	kev sib ntxiv
adjacent angles	الزوايا المتجاورة	邻角	鄰角	ob lub ces kaum sib npuab zoo sib xws
adjacent sides	الأضلاع المتجاورة	邻边	鄰邊	ob sab sib npuab zoo sib xws
after	بعد	在……之后；在……后面；在……以后	在……之後；在……後面；在……以後	tom qab
afternoon	بعد الظهر	下午	下午	tav su
algebra	الجبر	代数	代數	kev ntsuas zauv
algorithm	الحساب / النظام العشري / الأرقام العربية	算法；规则系统	演算法；規則系統	kev cai ntsuas cov zauv tsis muaj xaus
alternate exterior angles	الزوايا الخارجية المتبادلة	外错角	外錯角	cov ces kaum sab nraum
alternate interior angles	الزوايا الداخلية المتبادلة	内错角	內錯角	cov ces kaum sab hauv
angle	زاوية	角	角	ces kaum
angle bisector	منصف الزاوية	角平分线；分角线	角平分線；分角線	kab txiav ua ob lub ces kaum zoo sib xws
approximation	التقريب	近似值；略计	近似值；略計	kws yees
area	منطقة / مساحة	面积	面積	nrog dav
arithmetic sequence	المتتالية الحسابية	等差序列	等差序列	kev ntsuas zauv raws seem
array	المصفوفة	阵列；数组	陣列；數組	raws seem
Associative Property of Addition	خاصية تجميع حاصل الجمع	加法结合性质	加法結合性質	Kev sib ntxiv tshaj peb tug zauv mus raws seem li cas los tau tsuav tawm tib yam

KOREAN	SPANISH	TAGALOG	URDŪ	VIETNAMESE
A				
초과	arriba	sa itaas	سے زیادہ	ở trên, trên
예각	ángulo agudo	anggulong agudo	زاویہ حادّہ	góc nhọn
예각 삼각형	triángulo acutángulo	trinaggulong agudo	مثلث حادّہ	tam giác nhọn
더하기, 더하다	sumar	pagdaragdag	جوڑنا	cộng
가수	sumando	addend	مضاف	cộng thêm
덧셈	suma	pagdaragdag	اضافہ	tính cộng, phép cộng
접각	ángulos adyacentes	mga magkakatabing anggulo	زاویہ متصلہ	góc kề
접변	lados adyacentes	mga magkakatabing panig	خطوط متصلہ	các cạnh kề nhau
−후에	después	pagkatapos	کے بعد	sau
오후	tarde	hapon	سہ پہر	buổi chiều
대수학	álgebra	alhebra	الجبرا	đại số
연산	algoritmo	algoritmo	قواعد اعداد	thuật toán
외엇각	ángulos externos alternos	mga halinhinang panlabas na anggulo	متبادل زاویہ خارجہ	các góc ngoài xen kẽ
엇각	ángulos internos alternos	mga halinhinang panloob na anggulo	متبادل زاویہ داخلہ	các góc trong xen kẽ
각	ángulo	anggulo	زاویہ	góc
각의 이등분선	bisector del ángulo	bisector ng anggulo	زاویہ خط تنصیف	đường phân giác của góc
근사	aproximación	paghuhumigit-kumulang	تخمینہ لگانا	phép tính xấp xỉ
면적	área	lawak	رقبہ	diện tích, bề mặt
등차수열	secuencia aritmética	aritmetikang pagkakasunod-sunod	حسابی ترتیب	dãy số
배열	matriz	maghanay	صف بندی	dãy
덧셈의 결합 법칙	Propiedad asociativa de la suma	Pagsama-samahing Katangian ng Pagdaragdag	جمع کی تلازمی خصوصیت	Tính Chất Kết Hợp của Phép Cộng

Mathematics Vocabulary in Nine Languages

ENGLISH	ARABIC	CHINESE SIMPLIFIED	CHINESE TRADITIONAL	HMONG
Associative Property of Multiplication	خاصية تجميع حاصل الضرب	乘法结合性质	乘法結合性質	Kev sib khun tshaj peb tug zauv mus raws seem li cas los tau tsuav tawm tib yam
average	متوسط / معدل	平均；平均数；平均值	平均；平均數；平均值	qhov nruab nrab
B				
balance	وازن / عادل / توازن / موازنة	平衡；均衡	平衡；均衡	sib xws, seem, ruaj
bar graph	رسم بياني بالأعمدة	条形图	條形圖	duab kos kab
base	قاعدة / أساس	底（数）；基；基数	底（數）；基；基數	lub qab, hauv paus
base ten system	النظام العشري	十进制法	十進位法	kev ntsuas zauv raws kev tso tee
before	قبل	在……之前；在……之先	在……之前；在……之先	ua ntej
behind	خلف / وراء	在……之后	在……之後	lawv qab
below	أدنى / أسفل / تحت	在……以下；低于	在……以下；低於	hauv qab
beside	بجانب	在……旁边	在……旁邊	nyob ib sab
between	بين	在……之间	在……之間	nyob nruab nrab
bias	منحرف / مائل	偏差	偏差	kab tav zij
bisect	تنصيف	平分；等分	平分；等分	txiav ob sab zoo sib xws
borrowing	استعارة / اقتباس	借位	借位	txais
C				
calculator	حاسبة	计算器	計算器	lub nias zauv
calendar	تقويم	日历	日曆	ntawv teev hnub thiab hli
cancel	يلغي / إلغاء	约去；消去；删除	約去；消去；刪除	kos tawm
capacity	سعة / قدرة	容量	容量	puv, ntim taus
cardinal numbers	الأعداد الأولية	基数；纯数	基數；純數	cov zauv kos los sib tshuam
Celsius	منوي	摄氏	攝氏	Ntsuas kub thiab txias uas 0 yog txias khov, 100 yog hlab kub heev
cent	سنت	分（货币单位）	分（貨幣單位）	nyiaj npib liab
center	مركز / محور / وسط	中心	中心	nruab nrab

KOREAN	SPANISH	TAGALOG	URDŪ	VIETNAMESE
곱셈의 결합 법칙	Propiedad asociativa de la multiplicación	Pagsama-samahing Katangian ng Pagpaparami	ضرب کی تلازمی خصوصیت	Tính Chất Kết Hợp của Phép Nhân
평균	promedio	pangkaraniwan	اوسط	trung bình
B				
균형	balanza	balanse	میزان	sự cân bằng
막대그래프	gráfica de barras	talangguhit na trangka	بار گراف	biểu đồ dạng thanh, biểu đồ dạng cột
밑변	base	base	قاعدہ، خط اساسی	đường đáy, mặt đáy
십진법	sistema base diez	sampung bilang na sistema	خط اساسی عشری نظام	hệ thập phân
–이전	antes	bago ang	پہلے	trước, đằng trước
–뒤에	detrás	sa likod	پیچھے	đằng sau, phía sau
미만	debajo	sa ilalim	نیچے	dưới, ở dưới
–옆에	al lado	bukod sa	متصل	bên cạnh, gần
–사이	entre	sa pagitan ng	درمیان	ở giữa, giữa
치우침, 편의	sesgo	walang kinikilingan	آڑا	đường chéo, đường xiên
이등분	bisecar	hatiin	تنصیف کرنا	chia đôi, cắt đôi
차용	tomar prestado	humihiram	ادھار لینا	vay mượn (danh từ)
C				
계산기	calculadora	kalkulador	کلکولیٹر	máy tính
달력	calendario	kalendaryo	کلنڈر	lịch
약분	cancelar	kansela	منسوخ کرنا	khử, xoá bỏ, hủy bỏ
용량	capacidad	kapasidad	گنجائش	sức chứa, công suất, dung lượng
기수	números cardinales	kardinal na numero	اعداد وصفی	số từ chỉ số lượng
섭씨	Celsius	Celsius	سیلسیس	độ C
센트	centavo	sentimo	صد	xu
중심	centro	gitna	وسط	điểm giữa, trung điểm, tâm

Mathematics Vocabulary in Nine Languages

ENGLISH	ARABIC	CHINESE SIMPLIFIED	CHINESE TRADITIONAL	HMONG
Centigrade	درجة مئوية	摄氏温度计的；百分度的	攝氏溫度計的；百分度的	Ntsuas kub thiab txias uas 0 yog txias khov, 100 yog hlab kub heev
centimeter	سنتيمتر	厘米	公分	xeestismev
central angle	زاوية مركزية	圆心角	圓心角	ces kaum nruab nrab
century	قرن	世纪	世紀	100 xyoo
certain	مؤكد	已确定的；固定的	已確定的；固定的	tej yam, paub tseeb
chance	فرصة	机遇	機遇	muaj feem
change	يغير / تغيير	转换；变换；改变	轉換；變換；改變	hloov
chronological order	ترتيب زمني	按年月顺序排列	按年月順序排列	raws sij hawm
circle	دائرة	圆	圓	voj voog
circle graph	مخطط بياني دائري	饼图	圓形圖	duab kos ua voj voog
circumference	محيط الدائرة	圆周	圓周	puag ncig tag
clockwise	اتجاه عقارب الساعة	顺时针方向	順時針方向	khiav raws lub teev dhia
cluster	مجموعة إحصائية ثانوية	串；丛集；束	串；叢集；束	ib pab pawg
columns	أعمدة	列；纵行；柱	列；縱行；柱	cov seem
combinations	التوافيق	组合	組合	sau ua ke
common denominator	المقام المشترك	同分母；公分母	同分母；公分母	zauv hauv qab zoo tib yam
common fraction	كسر اعتيادي	普通分数；简分数	普通分數；簡分數	zauv faib zoo tib yam
common year	سنة بسيطة	平年	平年	xyoo zoo tib yam
Commutative Property of Addition	الخاصية التبادلية للجمع	加法交换性质	加法交換性質	Kev sib ntxiv ob tug zauv mus raws seem li cas los tau tsuav tawm tib yam
Commutative Property of Multiplication	الخاصية التبادلية للضرب	乘法交换性质	乘法交換性質	Kev sib khun ob tug zauv mus raws seem li cas los tau tsuav tawm tib yam
comparative bar graph	رسم بياني مقارن بالأعمدة	比较条形图	比較條形圖	duab kos kab sib piv
comparison symbol	رمز المقارنة	比较符号	比較符號	sib piv cim

KOREAN	SPANISH	TAGALOG	URDŪ	VIETNAMESE
섭씨	centígrado	Sentigrado	سنٹی گریڈ	độ C, bách phân
센티미터	centímetro	sentimetro	سنٹی میٹر	xentimet, xăng-ti-mét
중심각	ángulo central	panggitnang anggulo	وسطی زاویہ	góc giữa
1세기, 100	siglo	siglo	صدی	thế kỷ
약간의, 일정한	cierto	sigurado	یقینی	chắc chắn
우연	posibilidad	tsansa	موقع	cơ hội, sự may rủi, khả năng có thể
변화	cambio	ipalit	تبدیلی	thay đổi
연대순	orden cronológico	ayos ng pagkakasunods-sunod	سال کی ترتیب	theo trình tự thời gian
원	círculo	sirkulo	دائرہ	đường tròn, hình tròn
원 그래프	gráfica circular	talangguhit ng sirkulo	مدوّر گراف	biểu đồ hình tròn
원주	circunferencia	sirkumperensiya	محیط	chu vi, đường tròn
시계방향	en el sentido de las manecillas del reloj	pakanan	گھڑی کی سمت میں	theo chiều kim đồng hồ
집락, 집단	cúmulo	kumpol	اجتماع	tập hợp, nhóm
열	columnas	pila	کالم	các cột
조합	combinaciones	kombinasyon	امتزاج، اتصال	các tổ hợp, các tập hợp
공통분모	denominador común	panglahat na denominator	مشترک نسب نما	mẫu số chung, mẫu thức
상분수	fracción común	panglahat na hating-bilang	کسر عام	phân số chung
평년	año común	panglahat na taon	عام سال	năm thường (không phải năm nhuận)
덧셈의 교환 법칙	Propiedad conmutativa de la suma	Katangian ng Paglipat-lipatin sa Pagdaragdag	جمع کی مستبدل خصوصیت	Tính Chất Giao Hoán của Phép Cộng
곱셈의 교환 법칙	Propiedad conmutativa de la multiplicación	Katangian sa Paglipat-lipatin sa Pagpaparami	ضرب کی مستبدل خصوصیت	Tính Chất Giao Hoán của Phép Nhân
비교 막대 그래프	gráfica de barras comparativa	mapaghahambing na talangguhit na trangka	تقابلی بار گراف	biểu đồ dạng cột, biểu đồ thanh dùng để so sánh
비교 부호	símbolo de comparación	mapaghahambing na simbolo	موازناتی علامت	ký hiệu so sánh

Mathematics Vocabulary in Nine Languages

ENGLISH	ARABIC	CHINESE SIMPLIFIED	CHINESE TRADITIONAL	HMONG
compass	بوصلة / فرجار	罗盘；圆规（复数）	羅盤；圓規（複數）	lub taw kev
compatible numbers	الأعداد المتوافقة	相容数	相容數	cov zauv zoo sib xws
complement of an event	متممة ناتج	补事件	補事件	kev ntsuas zauv uas muaj ob yam sib txuam, xws li ob daim pib
complementary angles	زاويتان متتامتان	余角	餘角	ob lub ces kaum ntsuas muaj 90 feem pua
composite number	عدد مركب	复合数；合成数	複合數；合成數	tus zauv uas sib ob tug sib khun muaj uas tsis yog 1
compound event	ناتج مركب	复合事件	複合事件	siv tshaj ob yam los ntsuas zauv
compound interest	فائدة مركبة	复利；复利息	複利；複利息	paj tsub zaum no thiab yav tag los ua ke
concentric circles	دوائر متمركزة / دوائر متحدة المركز	同心圆	同心圓	cov voj voog muaj lub nruab plawv sib luag
cone	مخروط / شكل مخروطي	锥；圆锥（体）	錐；圓錐（體）	lub kheej kheej khoob ib tog me me ntse ntse
congruent	متطابق	全等	全等	zoo sib xws
consecutive number	أعداد متتالية	连续数；相邻数	連續數；相鄰數	zauv sib law liag
continuous data	معطيات مستمرة	连续数据	連續資料	lus txuas pes zws
coordinate graph	رسم بياني إحداثي	坐标图	座標圖	duab kos kab chaw tshuam
coordinate plane	سطح مستو إحداثي	坐标平面	座標平面	daim plag kos kab chaw tshuam
coordinates	إحداثيات	坐标	座標	cov chaw tshuam
corresponding angles	زوايا متناظرة	同位角；对应角	同位角；對應角	cov ces kaum sib npuab
corresponding parts	أجزاء متناظرة	对应部份	對應部份	cov yas sib npuab
count	عد / حساب	计数；点数；计算；清点	計數；點數；計算；清點	suav
count back	عد عكسي	倒数	倒數	suav rov qab
count on	يعتمد على	计数	計數	suav mus

KOREAN	SPANISH	TAGALOG	URDŪ	VIETNAMESE
컴퍼스	brújula	kompas	منحنی	com-pa, la bàn
양립 가능한 수	números compatibles	magkabagay na mga bilang	موافق اعداد	các số tương thích
사건의 여집합	complemento de un evento	magkakabagay na pangyayari	کسی واقعہ کا تکملہ	sự bù trừ của một biến cố
보각	ángulos complementarios	mga magkabagay na anggulo	زاویہ تکملہ	các góc bù
합성수	número compuesto	composite na numero	عدد مقسوم	số đa hợp, số hợp tử
복합사건	evento compuesto	tambalan na pangyayari	معاملہ مرکب	biến cố phức hợp
복리	interés compuesto	tambalan na interes	سود مرکب	lãi kép
동심원	círculos concéntricos	concentric na bilog	ہم مرکز دائرے	các đường tròn đồng tâm
원뿔	cono	kono	مخروط	hình nón
합동	congruente	kongruente	موافق	có cùng kích thước và hình dạng, đồng dạng
연속 수	número consecutivo	magkakasunod na numero	عدد متواتر	số liên tiếp
연속 자료	datos continuos	patuloy na datos	مسلسل ڈیٹا	dữ liệu liên tiếp, số liệu liên tiếp
좌표 그래프	gráfica de coordenadas	koordena na talangguhit	ہم نسق گراف	biểu đồ toạ độ
좌표평면	plano coordenado	koordenadang patag	مساوی سطح	mặt phẳng toạ độ
좌표	coordenadas	mga koordenada	ہم نسق	các tọa độ
동위각	ángulos correspondientes	mga magkabagay na anggulo	زاویہ مماثل	các góc đồng vị
동위부	partes correspondientes	mga magkabagay na bahagi	اجزائے مماثل	các phần tương ứng
세다	contar	bilang	شمار	đếm
거꾸로 세다	contar hacia atrás	bumilang pabalik	دوبارہ شمار کرنا	đếm ngược
의지하다, 기대하다	contar hacia adelante	magpatuloy sa pagbilang	گنتی کرنا	đếm với

Mathematics Vocabulary in Nine Languages

ENGLISH	ARABIC	CHINESE SIMPLIFIED	CHINESE TRADITIONAL	HMONG
counterclockwise	عكس اتجاه عقارب الساعة	逆时针方向	逆時針方向	kiv rov qab lub teev
counting numbers	أعداد حسابية	数数	數數	suav cov zauv
counting patterns	أنماط حسابية	点数图案；点数图样	點數圖案；點數圖樣	suav cov qauv
cross products	حاصل الضرب الموجه	交叉乘积	交叉乘積	kev siv cov zauv los ntsuas sib piv seb puas muaj tseeb thiab puas ntsuas tawm tib yam
cube	مكعب	正方体；立方；立方体	正方體；立方；立方體	lub nkev khoob muaj 6 sab
cubic unit	وحدة مكعبة	立方单位	立方單位	kev ntsuas nraws plaub sab sib luag zos
cup	قدح / كوب / فنجان	杯；杯体；求并运算	杯；杯體；求並運算	khob
customary unit	وحدة اعتيادية	惯例计量单位	慣例度量單位	kev ntsuas raws unit
cylinder	أسطوانة / شكل أسطواني	柱；圆柱体	柱；圓柱體	lub ntev kheej khoob

D

ENGLISH	ARABIC	CHINESE SIMPLIFIED	CHINESE TRADITIONAL	HMONG
data	معطيات / بيانات	数据	資料	ntaub ntawv
date	تاريخ	日期	日期	hnub
decade	عقد	十；十个一组；十年	十；十個一組；十年	kaum xyoo
decagon	مضلع عشاري / معشر الأضلاع	十边形	十邊形	lub muaj kaum sab thiab kaum lub ces kaum
decimal	عشري / كسر عشري	小数	小數	kev ntsuas zauv raws lub tee
decimal places	مراتب عشرية	小数位	小數位	cov chaw ntsuas teeb lub tee
decimal point	فاصلة عشرية / فاصلة الكسر العشري	小数点	小數點	ib tee twg
decimeter	ديسيمتر / عشرة سنتيمترات	分米	公寸；分米	ciaj ntsuas raws cov tee
decrease	تناقص / خفض	递减	遞減	lov kom tsawg, ua kom me, ua kom yau
degree	درجة	度；次	度；次	feem pua, qib
denominator	مقام الكسر	分母	分母	zauv hauv qab

KOREAN	SPANISH	TAGALOG	URDŪ	VIETNAMESE
반시계방향	en el sentido contrario a las manecillas del reloj	pakaliwa	ضدّ ساعت وار	ngược chiều kim đồng hồ
숫자 세기	números naturales	mga binibilang na numero	اعداد شمار	các số đếm
셈 형식	patrones de conteo	mga binibilang na pattern	گنتی کا طریقہ	các mô hình đếm
벡터곱, 외적	productos cruzados	cross products	متعلقہ مصنوعات	các tích số ngược nhau
세제곱, 정육면체	cubo	cube	مکعب	hình lập phương, hình khối
입방 단위	unidad cúbica	yunit ng cube	مکعبی اکائی	đơn vị bậc ba, đơn vị khối
컵	taza	tasa	پیالہ	chén, ly
도량 단위	unidad usual	customary na yunit	مروّجہ اکائی	đơn vị thường dùng
원기둥	cilindro	silindro	اسطوانہ	hình trụ

D

자료	datos	datos	ڈیٹا	số liệu, dữ liệu
날짜	fecha	petsa	تاریخ	ngày, thứ (trong tuần)
10년간	década	dekada	دہائی	thập kỷ, 10 năm
십각형	decágono	dekagono	دہ پہلو شکل	hình mười cạnh, hình thập giác
소수의	decimal	decimal	اعشاریہ	thập phân
소수자리	cifras decimales	desimal na lugar	مقامات اعشاریہ	vị trí thập phân
소수점	punto decimal	desimal na tuldok	نقطۂ اعشاریہ	điểm thập phân
데시미터	decímetro	decimetro	ڈیسی میٹر	đề-xi-mét
감소하다	disminuir	bawasan	تخفیف ہونا	giảm bớt, giảm
도, 차수	grado	grado	درجہ	độ
분모	denominador	pambahagi	نسب نما	mẫu số, mẫu thức

Mathematics Vocabulary in Nine Languages

ENGLISH	ARABIC	CHINESE SIMPLIFIED	CHINESE TRADITIONAL	HMONG
dependent events	النواتج التابعة	相关事件；相依事件；从属事	相關事件；相依事件；從屬事	cov nqe zauv uas ntsuas tawm zoo sib xws
diameter	قطر	直径	直徑	qhov nrog dav
difference	اختلاف / فرق	差	差	qhov sib txawv
digit	رقم	数字；数位	數字；數位	zauv
digital time	العصر الرقمي	数字时间	數位時間	sij hawm dhia zauv
dimension	بعد	次元；度（数）；维（数）//（复数）容积；面积；大小；规模；范围	次元；度（數）；維（數）//（複數）容積；面積；大小；規模；範圍	fab
direction	اتجاه	方向	方向	qhia kev
disjoint events	النواتج المنفصلة	不相交事件	不相交事件	cov nqe zauv uas ntsuas tawm tsis zoo sib xws
Distributive Property	الخاصية التوزيعية	分配律	分配律	Txoj kev khun zauv uas yog siv tau tshaj ob twg zauv sab hauv los khun nrog tus zauv sab nraum no xws li tias a(b + c) = ab + ac
divide	يقسم / قسمة / تقسيم	除	除	sib faib
dividend	المقسوم / حصة	被除数；股息	被除數；股息	tus zauv yuav raug muab faib
divisibility	قابلية القسمة	可除尽；整约性；整除性	可除盡；整約性；整除性	txoj kev faib kom txwm tsis seem
divisible	قابل للقسمة	可整除	可整除	faib tau txwm nkaus tsis tshuav seem
division	قسمة	除法	除法	kev sib faib
divisor	قاسم / مقسوم عليه	除数；除式；因子	除數；除式；因子	tus zauv siv los faib kom tsis seem
double-line graph	رسم بياني مزدوج الخطوط	双线图	雙線圖	daim duab kos cov khub kab
doubles	مضاعفات	倍数；两倍数	倍數；兩倍數	cov khub
dozen	دزينة / دستة	一打；十二个	一打；十二個	kaum ob
E				
edge	حد / طرف / حافة	棱；边	棱；邊	ntug
eight	ثمانية	八	八	yim
eighth	ثامن / ثُمن	第八	第八	qib yim
elapsed time	الوقت المستغرق	实耗时间	實耗時間	lub sij hawm ntsuas ntev li cas
eleventh	حادي عشر	第十一	第十一	qib kaum ib

KOREAN	SPANISH	TAGALOG	URDŪ	VIETNAMESE
종속 사건	eventos dependientes	mga umaasang pangyayari	متوسّل واقعات	các biến cố phụ thuộc
지름	diámetro	diyametro	قطر	đường kính
차, 나머지	diferencia	natirang bilang	تفریق	hiệu số, sai phân
숫자	dígito	bilang	عدد	chữ số
디지털 시간	hora digital	digital time	عددی وقت	giờ điện tử
차원	dimensión	dimensyon	بعد، حد	kích thước, kích cỡ
방향	dirección	direksyon	سمت	chiều, hướng
서로 소인 사건	eventos no relacionados	disjoint events	بے ربط واقعات	tách rời các sự kiện
분배 법칙	Propiedad distributiva	Katangiang Pamamahagi	تقسیمی واقعات	Tính Chất Phân Bổ
나누다	dividir	hatiin	تقسیم کرنا	chia
피제수	dividendo	dibidend	مقسوم	số bị chia
나뉘어떨어짐	divisibilidad	mahahati	تقسیم پذیری	tính chia hết
나뉘어떨어지는	divisible	maaaring hatiin	تقسیم پذیر	chia hết cho
나눗셈	división	paghahati	تقسیم	phép chia
제수	divisor	dibisor	مقسوم علیہ	số chia
이중선 그래프	gráfica de línea doble	doble-linyang talangguhit	دو خط والا گراف	biểu đồ 2 đường kẻ
곱, 갑절, 두 배	dobles	doble	دوبرے	các số gấp đôi, nhân đôi
12개, 다스	docena	dosena	درجن	tá (mười hai)
E				
모서리	borde	gilid	کنارہ	đỉnh
여덟	ocho	walo	آٹھ	tám
여덟번째	octavo	ikawalo	آٹھواں	thứ tám
경과 시간	tiempo transcurrido	lumapas na oras	قضاء شدہ وقت	thời gian trôi qua
열한번째	decimoprimero	ikalabing-isa	گیاربواں	thứ mười một

Mathematics Vocabulary in Nine Languages

ENGLISH	ARABIC	CHINESE SIMPLIFIED	CHINESE TRADITIONAL	HMONG
end point	نقطة النهاية	端点	端點	qhov kawg
equal groups	مجموعات متساوية	等组	等組	cov pawg sib npaug
equal parts	أجزاء متساوية	相等部份	相等部份	cov ntu sib luag
equal to	مساو لـ / يساوي	等于	等於	muaj tib yam li
equally likely	مرجح/محتمل بالتساوي	（事件发生的）均等机会；同样可能	（事件發生的）均等機會；同樣可能	muaj feem sib luag zos
equals	يساوي / كميات متعادلة	等号；等子	等號；等子	muaj li, sib luag, zoo tib yam li
equation	معادلة	方程式；等式	方程式；等式	nqe zauv
equiangular	متساوي الزوايا	等角的	等角的	tag nrho cov ces kaum sib luag zos
equilateral triangle	مثلث متساوي الأضلاع	等边三角形	等邊三角形	lub peb ces kaum khoob uas muaj peb sab
equivalent fractions	كسور متكافئة/متعادلة	等值分数	等值分數	faib kom sib luag
estimate	يقدر / تقدير / قيمة تقديرية	估计；估计量	估計；估計量	kwv yees
evaluate	يقيم / يقدر القيمة	求……值；计值	求……值；計值	soj ntsuam
even	متعادل / متساو / زوجي	偶数的；双数的	偶數的；雙數的	khub, sib txig
even number	عدد زوجي	偶数	偶數	zauv khub
evening	مساء / معادلة / مساواة	傍晚	傍晚	hmo ntuj
event	حدث / ناتج	事件	事件	koom txoos
expanded form	شكل ممدد / موسع	展开式	展開式	hloov kom loj
expanded notation	مجموعة رموز موسعة	展开式记数法	展開式記數法	faib cov zauv kom mus ua ntau tus
experiment	تجربة / اختبار	实验	實驗	sim kawm
experimental probability	الاحتمال التجريبي	实验概率	實驗概率	feem sim kawm
exponent	أس / دليل / القوة الجبرية	指数	指數	tus cim los yog tus zauv ua kom loj los yog nce
exponential expression	عبارة أسية	指数式；指数表示法	指數式；指數表示法	txoj kev teeb zauv uas muaj nce xws li tus e
expression	عبارة / تعبير	式；数式	式；數式	kev teeb zauv
exterior angle	زاوية خارجية	外角	外角	lub ces kaum sab nraum no

KOREAN	SPANISH	TAGALOG	URDŪ	VIETNAMESE
끝점	punto extremo	dulong tuldok	نقطۂ انتہا	điểm giới hạn, điểm kết thúc
동질 집단	grupos iguales	mga pare-parehong grupo	مساوی گروپس	các nhóm bằng nhau
같은 부분	partes iguales	mga pare-parehong parte	مساوی اجزا	các phần bằng nhau
−와 같다	igual a	pare-pareho sa	کے برابر	bằng, tương đương với
같은 확률로	igualmente probable	pare-pareho sa maaaring	تقریبا برابر	có khả năng bằng nhau, có thể bằng nhau
같다	es igual a	pareho sa	برابر برابر	bằng
방정식	ecuación	pantayan	مساوات	phương trình
등각의	equiangular	equiangular	مساوی الزاویہ	đều góc, đẳng giác
정삼각형	triángulo equilátero	equilateral na trianggulo	مثلث متساوی الاضلاع	tam giác đều
동치분수	fracciones equivalentes	mga magkatumbas na hating-bilang	مساوی کسور	các phân số bằng nhau
어림잡다	estimar	tantya	تخمینہ	ước lượng
−의 값을 구하다	evaluar	pahalagahan	تشخیص	định giá, đánh giá (động từ)
짝수의	par	tukol	جفت	chẵn
짝수	número par	tukol na bilang	جفت عدد	số chẵn
저녁	noche	gabi	شام	buổi tối
사건	evento	pangyayari	واقعہ	trường hợp, biến cố
전개형	forma desarrollada	pinalawak na anyo	توسیعی شکل	dạng mở rộng
전개 기호	notación desarrollada	pinalawak na pagtatala	توسیعی اشارات	phần chú thích mở rộng
실험, 시행	experimento	eksperimento	تجربہ	thí nghiệm, thử nghiệm
경험적 확률	probabilidad experimental	eksperimento na probabilidad	تجرباتی امکان	xác xuất thử nghiệm
지수	exponente	eksponente	قوت نما	số mũ
지수함수식	expresión exponencial	eksponensyal na pagpapahayag	قوت نمایانہ ترکیب	biểu thức số mũ
식	expresión	pagpapahayag	ترکیب	biểu thức
외각	ángulo externo	panlabas na anggulo	زاویہ خارجہ	góc ngoài

Mathematics Vocabulary in Nine Languages

ENGLISH	ARABIC	CHINESE SIMPLIFIED	CHINESE TRADITIONAL	HMONG
F				
face	وجه / سطح / جانب	面	面	sab nraum, sab xub ntiag, tus nqi
fact family	زمرة حقائق عددية	数组概念	數組概念	cov zauv uas khun tawm me tshaj plaws thiab faib tsis tau
factor	عامل / معامل	因子；因式；商	因子；因式；商	zauv siv los sib khnu
factor tree	شجرة المعامل	因子树形图；系统图法	因子樹形圖；系統圖法	teeb cov zauv uas siv los sib khun los zoo li tsob ntoo
Fahrenheit	فهرنهايت	华氏温度计；华氏温度计（的）	華氏溫度計；華氏溫度計（的）	txoj kev ntsuas txias txog 32 thiab kub txog 212
faster	أسرع	更快	更快	ceev dua
fastest	الأسرع	最快	最快	ceev heev tshaj
feet	أقدام	英尺（复数）	英尺（複數）	taws
fewer	أقل	更少	更少	tsawg dua
fewest	الأقل	最少	最少	tsawg heev tshaj
Fibonacci sequence	أعداد فيبوناتشي	费布纳西数列；费氏数列；斐波那契序列；黄金分割数列	費布納西數列；費氏數列；斐波那契序列；黃金分割數列	cov zauv uas tsis muaj xaus
fifth	خامس / خُمس	第五	第五	qib tsib
first	الأول	第一	第一	qib ib, ua ntej
flip	يقلب / قلب	翻转	翻轉	tig, dhia
fluid ounce	أوقية سائلة	液体盎司；液量盎司；液盎司	液體盎司；液量盎司；液盎司	ntsuas kua
foot	قدم / قاعدة	英尺（单数）	英尺（單數）	taw
formula	صيغة / معادلة / عبارة اصطلاحية	公式	公式	nqe zauv
fourth	رابع / رُبع	第四	第四	qib plaub
fraction	كسر	分数；分式	分數；分式	zauv sib faib, ib feem
fraction bar	خط الكسر	分数条形显示图	分數條形顯示圖	kev pib kawm faib zauv
freezing point	درجة التجمد	冰点；结冰点	冰點；結冰點	qib txias khov
frequency	تردد / تواتر / تكرر	频数；频率	頻數；頻率	pes tsawg zaus
frequency table	جدول التواتر	频数表	頻數表	kev teeb muaj pes tsawg zaus

KOREAN	SPANISH	TAGALOG	URDŪ	VIETNAMESE
F				
면	cara	patag	رخ	mặt, mặt trước, bề mặt
관계 있는 세 개의 숫자 모임	familia de operaciones	fact family	وجہى قدر	nhóm dữ kiện
인수	factor	paktora	جزو ضربى	thừa số
인수 트리	árbol de factores	puno ng paktora	شجر جزو ضربى	biểu đồ thừa số hình cây
화씨	Fahrenheit	Fahrenheit	فارن ہائٹ	độ F
더 빠른	más rápido	mabilis	تیز تر	nhanh hơn
가장 빠른	el más rápido	pinakamabilis	تیز ترین	nhanh nhất
피트	pies	piye	فٹ	feet
더 적은	menos cantidad	mas kaunti	کمتر	ít hơn
가장 적은	la menor cantidad	pinaka-kaunti	کمترین	ít nhất
피보나치 수열	secuencia de Fibonacci	Fibonacci sequence	فائبوناسى ترتیب	dãy Fibonacci
다섯번째	quinto	ikalima	پانچواں	thứ năm
첫번째	primero	ika-una	پہلا	thứ nhất
튀기다	voltear	flip	اچھالنا	búng, tung
액량 온스	onza fluida	likidong onsa	مائع اونس	ao-xơ lỏng
피트	pie	talampakan	فٹ	phút, foot
공식	fórmula	pormularyo	فارمولہ	công thức
네번째	cuarto	ika-apat	چوتھا	thứ bốn, thứ tư
분수	fracción	hating-bilang	کسر	phân số
가로선	barra de fracciones	hating-bilang na trangka	کسر نما	thanh phân số
어는 점	punto de congelamiento	sobrang panlalamig na tuldok	نقطۂ انجماد	điểm đông, điểm đóng băng
도수, 빈도	frecuencia	kadalasan	تعدّد	tần số
도수분포표	tabla de frecuencias	talaan ng kadalasan	جدول تعدّد	bảng tần số

Mathematics Vocabulary in Nine Languages

ENGLISH	ARABIC	CHINESE SIMPLIFIED	CHINESE TRADITIONAL	HMONG
full turn	دورة كاملة	全转；全旋转；全翻转；完整翻转	全轉；全旋轉；全翻轉；完整翻轉	tig tag nrho
function	دالة / وظيفة	函数	函數	kev teeb ob pawg zauv kom los sib phim
function rule	قانون الدالة	函数律	函數律	txoj cai siv cov zauv mus ntsuas kom tawm tau cov zauv li cas

G

ENGLISH	ARABIC	CHINESE SIMPLIFIED	CHINESE TRADITIONAL	HMONG
gallon	جالون	加仑	加侖	thoob, taub
geometric sequence	متتالية هندسية	等比序列	等比序列	zauv ntsuas mus sib law liag
geometric solid	مجسم هندسي	几何立体模型；几何实体	幾何立體模型；幾何實體	cov xwm uas tsis khoob
geometry	الهندسة	几何；几何学	幾何；幾何學	kev ntsuas zauv raws tej xwm, tej tee, tej kab, tej ces kaum thiab teb chaw
gram	جرام	克	克	kev ntsuas qhov nyhav
graph	رسم بياني / خط بياني	图像；图形；图表	圖像；圖形；圖表	duab kos
greater	أكبر	更大	更大	ntau dua, siab dua, loj dua
greater than	أكبر من	大于	大於	ntau dua, siab dua, loj dua
greatest	الأكبر	最大	最大	ntau heev tshaj, siab heev tshaj, loj heev tshaj
greatest common factor (GCF)	العامل المشترك الأكبر	最大公因子；最大公因子	最大公約數；最大公因數	tus zauv loj tshaj plaws
groups of	مجموعات من	……组	……組	cov pab pawg

H

ENGLISH	ARABIC	CHINESE SIMPLIFIED	CHINESE TRADITIONAL	HMONG
half	نصف / شطر	半；一半	半；一半	ib nrab
half past	إلا ثلاثين دقيقة	过半；过半点	過半；過半點	peb caug feeb dhau
half turn	نصف دورة	半旋转；转体半周	半旋轉；轉體半周	tig ib nrab
heavier	أثقل	更重	更重	nyhav dua
heaviest	الأثقل	最重	最重	nyhav heev tshaj
height	ارتفاع	高；高度	高；高度	qhov siab
hexagon	مسدس / شكل سداسي	六边形	六邊形	lub xwm muaj rau lub ces kaum thiab rau sab

KOREAN	SPANISH	TAGALOG	URDŪ	VIETNAMESE
완전 회전	giro completo	full turn	مکمل موڑ	trọn vòng
함수	función	gawain	تفاعل	hàm số
함수 법칙	regla de función	patakaran ng gawain	اصول تفاعل	quy tắc hàm số

G

KOREAN	SPANISH	TAGALOG	URDŪ	VIETNAMESE
갤런	galón	galon	گیلن	Galông, gallon
등비수열	secuencia geométrica	heometriyang pagkakasunod-sunod	جیومیٹریائی ترتیب	chuỗi hình học, dãy hình học
기하입체	sólido geométrico	hemoteriyang solido	جیو میٹریائی ٹھوس	hình học ba chiều
기하학	geometría	heometriya	جیومیٹری	hình học
그램	gramo	gramo	گرام	gam
그래프	gráfica	talangguhit	گراف	đồ thị, biểu đồ
더 큰	mayor	mas malaki	بڑا	lớn hơn
−보다 큰	mayor que	mas malaki kumpara sa	نسبتا بڑا	lớn hơn
가장 큰, 최대	el mayor	pinakamalaki	سب سے بڑا	lớn nhất
최대공약수	máximo común divisor (MCD)	pinakamalaking panglahat na paktora	سب سے بڑا مشترک جزو ضربی	thừa số chung lớn nhất
−군	grupos de	grupo ng	کا مجموعہ	các nhóm của

H

KOREAN	SPANISH	TAGALOG	URDŪ	VIETNAMESE
반	medio	kalahati	نصف	một nửa, nửa
절반이 지난	y media	kahati matapos ang	گزرا ہوا نصف	rưỡi (giờ)
반회전	medio giro	kalahating liko	نصف موڑ	nửa vòng
더 무거운	más pesado	mas mabigat	نسبتا بڑا	nặng hơn
가장 무거운	el más pesado	pinakamabigat	سب سے بڑا	nặng nhất
높이, 키	altura	taas	قد	chiều cao
육각형	hexágono	heksagono	مسدّس	hình sáu cạnh, hình lục giác

Mathematics Vocabulary in Nine Languages

ENGLISH	ARABIC	CHINESE SIMPLIFIED	CHINESE TRADITIONAL	HMONG
histogram	مخطط درجي	组织图；直方图；矩形图	組織圖；直方圖；矩形圖	duab kos qhia seb pes tsawg zaus
horizontal	أفقي	水平线；水平面；水平；水平的	水平線；水平面；水平；水平的	rov tav toj
horizontal axis	محور أفقي	水平轴	水平軸	txoj kab tav toj
hour	ساعة	小时	小時	teev
hundred thousands	مئات الآلاف	十万	十萬	ib puas phav
hundreds	مئات	百	百	pua
hundredth	مئة / جزء من المئة	第一百；第一百个；第一百号；百分之一	第一百；第一百個；第一百號；百分之一	pua

I

ENGLISH	ARABIC	CHINESE SIMPLIFIED	CHINESE TRADITIONAL	HMONG
identical	متطابق	全等；恒等	全等；恆等	zoo tib yam
identity element	عنصر محايد	单位元	單位元	tus zauv uas tsis hloov
Identity Property of Addition	الخاصية المحايدة للجمع	加法恒等性质	加法恆等性質	kev ntsuas zauv uas yog ntxiv 0 rau tus zauv twg ces yeej muaj li tus zauv ntawd xwb
Identity Property of Multiplication	الخاصية المحايدة للضرب	乘法恒等性质	乘法恆等性質	kev ntsuas zauv uas yog khun 1 rau tus zauv twg ces yeej muaj li tus zauv ntawd xwb
impossible	مستحيل	不可能的	不可能的	muaj tsis tau
improper fraction	كسر غير حقيقي	假分数	假分數	nqe zauv uas tus zauv saum toj loj dua tus hauv qab
in back of	خلف	在……背面	在……背面	sab nraum qab ntawm
in front of	أمام	在……正面	在……正面	sab xub ntiag ntawm
inch	بوصة	英寸	英寸	nti
increase	زيادة	递增；增加	遞增；增加	ntxiv, nce
independent events	نواتج مستقلة	独立事件	獨立事件	cov nqe zauv uas tsis sib muaj feem xyuam
infinity	اللانهائية	无限（大）；无穷（大）	無限（大）；無窮（大）	mus tsis txawj kawg
inside	داخل	内部；内面；里面	內部；內面；裡面	sab hauv
integers	الأعداد الصحيحة	整数	整數	cov zauv (negative, positive thiab 0)
interest	فائدة	利息	利息	paj laum, txaus siab

KOREAN	SPANISH	TAGALOG	URDŪ	VIETNAMESE
히스토그램	histograma	histogramo	مستطیلی ترسیم	biểu đồ
수평	horizontal	pahiga	افقی	nằm ngang, chiều ngang
수평축	eje horizontal	pahigang axis	افقی محور	trục hoành
시간	hora	oras	گھنٹہ	giờ
수십만	cientos de miles	daang libo	سیکڑوں ہزار	hàng trăm ngàn
수백	cientos	daan	سیکڑوں	hàng trăm
백번째	centésima	ika-isang daan	سوال	thứ một trăm

I

KOREAN	SPANISH	TAGALOG	URDŪ	VIETNAMESE
동일한	idéntico	identikal	متماثل	đồng nhất
항등원소, 단위원소	elemento de identidad	pagkakakilanlan na elemento	تماثلی عنصر	yếu tố phân tử đồng nhất thức
덧셈의 항등성	Propiedad de identidad de la suma	Katangian ng Pagkakakilanlan ng Pagdaragdag	جمع کی تماثلی خصوصیت	Tính Chất Đồng Nhất của Phép Cộng
곱셈의 항등성	Propiedad de identidad de la multiplicación	Katangian Pagdaragdag ng Pagpaparami	ضرب کی تماثلی خصوصیت	Tính Chất Đồng Nhất của Phép Nhân
불가능한, 무리한	imposible	di-makatotohanan	ناممکن	không thể xảy ra
가분수	fracción impropia	di-wastong hating-bilang	کسر غیر واجب	phân số không thực sự
−의 뒤에	detrás de	sa likod ng	کے پیچھے	phía sau của
−의 앞에	delante de	sa harap ng	کے سامنے	phía trước của
인치	pulgada	pulgada	انچ	insơ
증가하다	aumentar	pagtaas	بڑھوتری	tăng lên, tăng
독립사건	eventos independientes	mga di-umaasang pangyayari	آزادانہ واقعات	các biến cố độc lập
무한대	infinito	kawalang katapusan	غیر محدود	vô cực, vô tận
내부	dentro	loob	اندر	bên trong, vào trong
정수	enteros	mga pambuong bilang	اعداد صحیح	số nguyên
이자	interés	interes	سود	lãi

Mathematics Vocabulary in Nine Languages

ENGLISH	ARABIC	CHINESE SIMPLIFIED	CHINESE TRADITIONAL	HMONG
interior angle	زاوية داخلية	内角	內角	lub ces kaum sab hauv
International System of Units	النظام الدولي للوحدات (الأساسية)	国际计量单位制	國際度量衡單位制	Kev ntsuas raws qhov ntev, qhov nyhav, lub teev, qhov kub thiab txias, muaj kua npaum cas thoob teb chaws
intersect	قاطع / تقاطع / نقطة تقاطع	相交	相交	sib tshuam
intersecting lines	خطوط متقاطعة	相交线	相交線	cov kab sib tshuam
inverse operations	عمليات عكسية	逆运算	逆運算	ob txoj kev ntsuas zauv sib txawv xws li sib ntxiv thiab sib rho
irrational numbers	الأعداد اللامنطقية (الصماء)	无理数	無理數	cov zauv uas faib tawm tsis txawj xaus
isosceles triangle	مثلث متساوي الساقين	等腰三角形	等腰三角形	lub muaj peb ces kaum uas ob sab sib luag

K

ENGLISH	ARABIC	CHINESE SIMPLIFIED	CHINESE TRADITIONAL	HMONG
Kelvin	وحدة كلفن	绝对温标; 开氏温标	絕對溫標; 開氏溫標	ib txoj kev ntsuas kub thiab txias
kilogram	كيلوجرام	公斤；千克	公斤；千克	ib txoj kev ntsuas kua txog uas yog 1000 gram
kilometer	كيلومتر	公里	公里	ib txoj kev ntsuas raws mev uas yog 1000 mev

L

ENGLISH	ARABIC	CHINESE SIMPLIFIED	CHINESE TRADITIONAL	HMONG
large	كبير	大；大的	大；大的	loj
larger	أكبر	更大	更大	loj dua
largest	الأكبر	最大	最大	loj heev tshaj
last	آخر / أخير	最后的；最末的；最近的；持久；经久	最後的；最末的；最近的；持久；經久	kawg, kav ntev
leap year	سنة كبيسة	闰年	閏年	xyoo uas muaj hnub tshaj
least	الأصغر	最小的；最少的	最小的；最少的	tsawg kawg

KOREAN	SPANISH	TAGALOG	URDŪ	VIETNAMESE
내각	ángulo interno	panloob na anggulo	زاویۂ داخلہ	góc trong
국제 단위계	Sistema internacional de unidades	International System of Units	اکائیوں کا بین الاقوامی نظام	Hệ Thống Đơn Vị Đo Lường Quốc Tế
교차	intersecar	pagbagtas	تنصیب کرنا	giao nhau, phân cắt
상관선	líneas intersecantes	bumabagtas na mga guhit	خطوط متقاطع	các đường thẳng giao nhau
역연산	operaciones inversas	mga kabaligtaran na operasyon	عمل معکوس	các phép toán nghịch đảo
무리수	números irracionales	iasyunal na numoro	اعداد غیر ناطق	các số vô tỷ
이등변 삼각형	triángulo isósceles	isosceles na trianggulo	مثلث متساوی الساقین	tam giác cân
K				
절대 온도	Kelvin	Kelvin	کیلون	Kilôoát giờ
킬로그램	kilogramo	kilogramo	کلو گرام	kilôgam
킬로미터	kilómetro	kilometro	کلو میٹر	kilômét
L				
큰	grande	malaki	بڑا	rộng, lớn
더 큰	más grande	mas malaki	نسبتا بڑا	rộng hơn, lớn hơn
가장 큰	el más grande	pinakamalaki	سب سے بڑا	rộng nhất, lớn nhất
말, 끝	último	huli	آخری	cuối cùng
윤년	año bisiesto	taong bistenyo	سال کبیسہ	năm nhuận
최소	menor	pinakamaliit	کمترین	ít nhất

Mathematics Vocabulary in Nine Languages

ENGLISH	ARABIC	CHINESE SIMPLIFIED	CHINESE TRADITIONAL	HMONG
least common denominator (LCD)	المقام المشترك الأصغر	最小公分母	最小公分母	tus zauv hauv qab uas me tshaj plaws thaum si
least common multiple (LCM)	المضاعف المشترك الأصغر (أو البسيط)	最小公倍数	最小公倍數	tus zauv hauv qab mes tshaj plaws uas ob tug zauv saum toj khun muaj
left	يسار / أيسر	左；左侧；左方	左；左側；左方	sab laug
length	الطول	长；长度；长短	長；長度；長短	qhov ntev
less	أقل / أصغر	更小的；较小的；更少的；较少的	更小的；較小的；更少的；較少的	tsawg, me
less than	أقل من / أصغر من	小于；少于	小於；少於	tsawg dua, me dua
lighter	أخف / أبسط	更轻的	更輕的	sib dua
lightest	الأخف / الأبسط	最轻的	最輕的	sib heev tshaj
likelihood of events	احتمالية النواتج	事件的可能性	事件的可能性	feem kwv yees tau
likely	محتمل / مرجح	可能的	可能的	feem
line	خط	线；行	線；行	kab
line graph	رسم بياني خطي	线图	線圖	duab kos kab
line of symmetry	خط التماثل	对称线	對稱線	kab zoo sib xws
line plot	مخطط بياني خطي	线图	線圖	duab kos kab zauv
liter	لتر	（容量单位）升	（容量單位）升	ntsuas qhov puv raws liter
longer	أطول	更长	更長	ntev dua
longest	الأطول	最长	最長	ntev heev tshaj
lowest terms	المقدار الأصغر للكسر	最简分数	最簡分數	cov zauv me tshaj plaws, qis tshaj plaws
M				
mass	كتلة / إجمالي / كلي	质量	質量	ntsuas qhov puv, nyhav, loj ntawm ib yam
mean	متوسط	平均（值）；平均数；中数	平均（值）；平均數；中數	qhov nruab nrab ntawm cov zauv
measure	مقياس	计量；测量；尺寸；尺度；量；分量；测度；计量法；计量单位；约数；量数	計量；測量；尺寸；尺度；量；分量；測度；度量法；計量單位；約數；量數	ntsuas

KOREAN	SPANISH	TAGALOG	URDŪ	VIETNAMESE
최소공분모	mínimo común denominador (mcd)	pinakamaliit na panglahat ng numerong nasa ilalim ng hating-bilang	کمترین مشترک نسب نما	mẫu số chung nhỏ nhất
최소공배수	mínimo común múltiplo (mcm)	pinakamaliit na panglahat na multiplo	کمترین مشترک اضعاف	bội số chung nhỏ nhất
왼쪽	izquierda	kaliwa	بایاں	phía trái, bên trái
길이	longitud	haba	عرض	độ dài, chiều dài
더 적은	menos	kaunti	کم	ít hơn
−보다 더 적은	menos que	mas kaunti kumpara sa	سے کم	nhỏ hơn
더 가벼운	más liviano	magaan	نسبتا ہلکا	sáng hơn, nhẹ hơn
가장 가벼운	el más liviano	pinakamagaan	سب سے ہلکا	sáng nhất, nhẹ nhất
사건 가능성	probabilidad de eventos	maaaring pagkakapareho ng mga pangyayari	واقعات کا امکان	khả năng có thể xảy ra các biến cố
확률이 있는	probable	maaari	امکان	có thể xảy ra
선	línea	guhit	خط	đường thẳng, vạch
선 그래프	gráfica lineal	talangguhit na guhit	خطی گراف	đồ thị đường thẳng
대칭선	eje de simetría	guhit ng simetriya	خط تشاکل	đường đối xứng
선작도	diagrama de puntos	guhit na mapa	لائن پلاٹ	biểu đồ đường thẳng
리터	litro	litro	لیٹر	lít
더 긴	más largo	mas mahaba	نسبتا لمبا	dài hơn
가장 긴	el más largo	pinakamahaba	سب سے لمبا	dài nhất
기약	terminos mínimos	pinakamababang termino	سب سے کم ترین مقدار	các số hạng nhỏ nhất
M				
무게, 질량	masa	masa/bulto	ذخیره	khối lượng
평균, 평균값	media	mean	حقیر	trung bình
측도, 약수	medir	sukat	پیمائش	ước số, đo (động từ)

Mathematics Vocabulary in Nine Languages

ENGLISH	ARABIC	CHINESE SIMPLIFIED	CHINESE TRADITIONAL	HMONG
measure of central tendency	مقياس الميل المركزي	集中量数；趋中量数	集中量數；趨中量數	kev ntsuas lub plawv los yog qhov nruab nrab
median	متوسط / مستقيم متوسط / عدد متوسط	中位数；中线	中位數；中線	tus zauv nruab nrab ntawm cov zauv
medium	وسيط / وسط / متوسط	间的；中等中数；平均；平均数；介质；中的	間的；中等中數；平均；平均數；介質；中的	qhov nruab nrab, lub plawv
mental computation	الحسابات العقلية	心算法	心算法	sib hlwb los ntsuas
meter	متر / عداد / جهاز قياس	测量仪表，计量器计；表 // (= metre) 米	測量儀錶，計量器計；表 // (= metre) 公尺	ntsuas qhov sib deb
metric system	النظام المتري	公制；米制	公制；米制	kev ntsuas qhov sib deb
metric unit	الوحدة المترية	十进制单位；公制单位	十進制單位；公制單位	ntsuas qhov sib deb raws unit
middle	وسط / أوسط / منتصف	中央；正中；中间；中部	中央；正中；中間；中部	qhov nruab nrab, lub plawv
midnight	منتصف الليل	午夜	午夜	ib tag hmo
mile	ميل	英里；哩	英里；哩	ntsuas qhov sib deb
milligram	ملليجرام	毫克	毫克	ntsuas kua
millimeter	ملليمتر	毫米	毫米	ntsuas qhov sib deb
millions	ملايين	百万	百萬	laab laab
minus	ناقص / سالب	负；负（的）；负数；负量；负号；减号；减	負；負（的）；負數；負量；負號；減號；減	rho, tshem
minute	دقيقة	分钟	分鐘	feeb
mixed number	عدد كسري: عدد صحيح وكسر	带分数	帶分數	zauv sib txuam
mode	نمط / نسق	众数	眾數	tus zauv tshwm ntau tshaj, yam tshwm sim ntau zaus
month	شهر	月；月份	月；月份	hli
more	أكثر	更多的；较多的	更多的；較多的	tshaj, ntau dua
morning	صباح	早晨；早上；上午	早晨；早上；上午	sawv ntxov
most	الأكثر / الأقصى	最多的；最大的；最高的；大部份；大多数	最多的；最大的；最高的；大部份；大多數	feem ntau, tshaj
multiple	مضاعف	倍数	倍數	ob peb qho, ob peb yam
multiplication	الضرب / المضاعفة	乘法	乘法	kev khun zauv
multiplication table	جدول الضرب	乘法表	乘法表	ntawv teev cov zauv khun

KOREAN	SPANISH	TAGALOG	URDŪ	VIETNAMESE
중심경향성의 측도	medida de tendencia central	sukat ng hilig na mapagitna	مرکزی رجحان کی پیمائش	đo xu hướng trọng tâm
중앙값	mediana	panggitna	وسطی	trung tuyến
중위, 중간	medio	midyum	اوسط	trung bình
암산	cálcuto mental	mentalal na komputasyon	دماغی جمع تفریق	tính nhẩm
미터	metro	metro	میٹر	mét
미터법	sistema métrico	metrikong sistema	میٹرک نظام	hệ mét
계량 단위	unidad métrica	yunit na metriko	میٹرک اکائی	đơn vị mét
중간, 평균	medio	gitna	درمیانی	giữa, ở giữa
한밤중	medianoche	hatinggabi	آدھی رات	nửa đêm
마일	milla	milya	میل	dặm
밀리그램	miligramo	milligramo	ملی گرام	miligam
밀리미터	milímetro	millimetro	ملی میٹر	milimét
수백만	millones	milyon	لاکھوں	hàng triệu
–	menos	bawas	منفی	âm, trừ
분	minuto	minuto	منٹ	phút
혼합수	número mixto	pinaghalong bilang	عدد مخلوط	số hỗn hợp
모드, 최빈수, 최빈값	moda	mode	طرز	phương thức
달	mes	buwan	ماہ	tháng
더 많은, 여분의	más	marami	نسبتا زیاده	hơn, nhiều hơn
아침	mañana	umaga	صبح	buổi sáng
가장 큰, 최대량	mayoría	pinaka	سب سے زیاده	nhiều nhất
배수, 중, 중복	múltiplo	multiplo	کثیر العناصر	bội số
승법, 곱셈	multiplicación	pagpaparami	اضعاف	phép tính nhân
곱셈표	tabla de multiplicación	talaan ng pagpaparami	جدول ضرب، پہاڑه	bảng cửu chương

Mathematics Vocabulary in Nine Languages

ENGLISH	ARABIC	CHINESE SIMPLIFIED	CHINESE TRADITIONAL	HMONG
multiply	يضرب / يضاعف	乘	乘	khun zauv
mutually exclusive	يحتمل إجابة واحدة صحيحة	互斥	互斥	ob yam tsis muaj tseeb tiag
N				
nearer to	أقرب إلى	更接近于	更接近於	ze rau
nearest ten	لأقرب عشرة	未满 10 的数以 10 计算；把小数点的数进位到整数	未滿 10 的數以 10 計算；把小數點的數進位到整數	ze heev tshaj rau kaum
negative number	عدد سالب	负数	負數	tus zauv negative, tus zauv tsis zoo/tsis muaj
net	صافي	净（值）	淨（值）	tawm, seem, muaj
nickel	نيكل	五分镍币	五分鎳幣	nyiaj tsib cent
night	الليل	晚上	晚上	hmo ntuj
ninth	تاسع / تُسع	第九	第九	qib cuaj
nonexample	غير نموذجي	反例	反例	ua tsis tau qauv
noon	الظهيرة	中午；正午	中午；正午	tav su
number	عدد / رقم	数；数目；数字；数额	數；數目；數字；數額	zauv
number line	خط الأعداد	数线	數線	kab zauv
number sentence	جملة عددية	数字句型	數字句型	nqe zauv
numeral	عددي / رقمي	数的；数字的	數的；數字的	zauv
numerator	بسط / صورة الكسر	分子	分子	tus zauv saum toj
O				
oblique	مائل / منحرف	斜的	斜的	tsis ncaj, tsis raws seem, zij, nkhaus
obtuse angle	زاوية منفرجة	钝角	鈍角	lub ces kaum loj dua 90 thiab me dua 180
obtuse triangle	مثلث منفرج الزوايا	钝角三角形	鈍角三角形	lub xwm peb sab uas muaj ib lub ces kaum loj dua 90 thiab me dua 180
octagon	مثمن / مضلع ثماني الأضلاع	八边形	八邊形	lub xwm muaj yim sab thiab yim lub ces kaum
odd	فردي	奇数的；单（数）的；奇数号的	奇數的；單（數）的；奇數號的	khib, txawv
odd number	عدد فردي	奇数	奇數	zauv khib

KOREAN	SPANISH	TAGALOG	URDŪ	VIETNAMESE
곱하다	multiplicar	pagparami	ضرب کرنا	nhân (động từ)
서로 배반적인	mutuamente excluyentes	mutual na ekskulibo	باہم متناقض	loại trừ lẫn nhau
N				
−에 더 근접한	más cerca a	malapit sa	سے قریب تر	gần hơn với
가장 근접한 10	decena más cercana	pinakamalapit na sampu	قریب ترین دس	mười gần nhất
음수	número negativo	negatibong bilang	عدد منفی	số âm
최종	neto	neto	میزان	mạng
5센트 동전	moneda de cinco centavos	nikel	نکل	đồng 5 xu, niken
밤	noche	gabi	رات	buổi đêm, buổi tối
아홉번째	noveno	ikasiyam	نواں	thứ chín
비예	contraejemplo	di-halimbawa	بے مثال	không phải là ví dụ mẫu
정오	mediodía	tanghali	دوپہر	buổi trưa, trưa
수	número	bilang	عدد	số
수직선	recta numérica	guhit ng bilang	عدد خط	dãy số
숫자와 연산기호로	sentencia numérica	bilang na pangungusap	عدد جملہ	đánh số câu (động từ), câu có chữ số
숫자(의)	numeral	numeral	عددی	chữ số (tính từ)
분자	numerador	pambilang	شمار کنندہ	tử số
O				
사선	oblicuo	pahilis	آڑا	góc 45 độ
둔각	ángulo obtuso	anggulong bika	زاویۂ منفرجہ	góc tù
둔각삼각형	triángulo obtusángulo	trianggulong bika	مثلث منفرجہ	tam giác tù
팔각형	octágono	okagono	مثمن	hình bát giác, hình tám cạnh
홀수의	impar	butal	طاق	lẻ
홀수	número impar	bilang na may butal kapag pinagdalawa	طاق عدد	số lẻ

Mathematics Vocabulary in Nine Languages

ENGLISH	ARABIC	CHINESE SIMPLIFIED	CHINESE TRADITIONAL	HMONG
on top of	أعلى	在……的顶部；在……的顶端；在……上	在……的頂部；在……的頂端；在……上	nyob saum toj ntawm
ones	آحاد	（若干个）一；（以）一（为单位计数）	（若干個）一；（以）一（為單位計數）	ib
operations	عمليات	运算	運算	kev siv zauv
opposite sides	الأضلاع المتقابلة	对边	對邊	ob sab ntug tig rov sib ntsia
opposites	متقابلات	（直角三角形中角的）对边	（直角三角形中角的）對邊	cov rov sib ntsia, cov sib rov qab
order	ترتيب	顺序；序；次序；阶；级	順序；序；次序；階；級	raws seem
order of operations	ترتيب العمليات	运算顺序	運算順序	raws kev siv zauv
ordered pair	زوج مرتب	序偶	序偶	ob tug zauv sau kom ib tug ua ntej ib tug los yog loj/me dua ib tug
ordinal numbers	الأعداد الترتيبية	序数	序數	cov zauv uas teev qhia thib
orientation	توجيه	排列方向；取向；定位	排列方向；取向；定位	kev txawb, kev teeb
origin	الأصل: نقطة تقاطع محاور الإحداثيات	原点	原點	hauv paus, pib
ounce	أوقية	盎司	盎司	ntsuas kev nyhav ntawm hmoov thiab kua
outcome	ناتج	结果	結果	tawm li cas, ntsuas tau li cas
outlier	القيمة الأبعد عن المتوسط	异常值；极端数；离开本体的部份；分离物	異常值；極端數；離開本體的部份；分離物	neeg los yog yam nyob los yog npuab sab nrauv
outside	خارجي	外部；外面；外侧	外部；外面；外側	nraum zoov, sab nrauv
over	فوق / أعلى	越过；在……的上面；以上	越過；在……的上面；以上	saum toj, tshaj, khwb
P				
pair	زوج	一对；一双；对偶	一對；一雙；對偶	ib khub, ib txwm
palindrome	رقم يُقرأ طردًا وعكسًا	回文序列；回文结构；回文对称	回文序列；回文結構；回文對稱	nqe lus los yog nqe zauv uas nyeem tau mus tau los
parallel	متواز	平行	平行	raws seem rov tav toj

KOREAN	SPANISH	TAGALOG	URDŪ	VIETNAMESE
…에 더하여	arriba de	sa itaas ng	کے سرے پر	trên đỉnh của, ở phía trên của
일의 자리의 수	unidades	isa	ایک	hàng đơn vị
사칙연산	operaciones	mga operasyon	افعال	các phép tính, phép toán
대변	lados opuestos	magkasalungat na panig	سمت مخالف	các cạnh đối diện
반대편	opuestos	mga kasalungat	متضادات	đối nhau
순서, 계, 차	orden	ayos	ترتیب	bậc, thứ tự
연산 순서	orden de operaciones	ayos ng mga operasyon	افعال کی ترتیب	thứ tự của các phép toán
순서쌍, 순서짝	par ordenado	isinaayos na pares	مرتب کرده جوڑا	cặp số sắp xếp theo thứ tự
순서수	números ordinales	ordinal na numero	اعداد توصیفی	các số thứ tự
향	orientación	orientasyon	سمت بندی	sự định hướng, hướng
원점	origen	pinagmulan	ماخذ	gốc
온스	onza	onsa	اونس	aoxơ, ounce
결과	resultado	kinabukasan	ماحصل	kết luận, kết quả
특이값	valor lejano	outlier	منفصل حصه	nằm ngoài, ở ngoài
외측	afuera	labas	باہر	bề ngoài, bên ngoài
초과	sobre	sobra	زیاده	lên trên, bên trên, hơn
P				
쌍	par	pares	جوڑا	đôi, cặp
회문	palíndromo	palindrome	مقلوب مستوی	đọc xuôi ngược đều giống nhau
평행	paralelo	magkahilera	متوازی	song song

Mathematics Vocabulary in Nine Languages

ENGLISH	ARABIC	CHINESE SIMPLIFIED	CHINESE TRADITIONAL	HMONG
parallel lines	مستقيمات متوازية	平行线	平行線	cov kab raws seem rov tav toj
parallelogram	متوازي الأضلاع	平行四边形	平行四邊形	lub xwm muaj plaub sab uas ob sab ntug tav toj
parentheses	جمل اعتراضية	括号	括號	ob tug cim ntug xov tej lus/zauv
partial product	حاصل جزئي	部分乘积	部分乘積	ib txhia zauv ntawm ib nqe zauv twg coj los sib khun
pattern	نموذج / نمط / مخطط / شكل	图案；图样	圖案；圖樣	qauv
pentagon	مخمس / شكل خماسي الأضلاع	五边形	五邊形	lub xwm muaj tsib sab thiab tsib lub ces kaum
percent	بالمائة	百分比；百分率	百分比；百分率	feem pua
perfect square	مربع تام	完全平方	完全平方	tus zauv uas luaj tib yam li ob npaug ntawm lwm tus zauv
perimeter	محيط	周长；周界	周長；周界	qhov puag ncig
permutation	التبدلة	排列	排列	txoj kev sib hloov chaw rau cov zauv/yam dab tsi
perpendicular	عمودي / متعامد	垂线；垂直（于）	垂線；垂直（於）	seem rov ntsug
perpendicular bisector	شعاع متعامد	垂直平分线；中垂线	垂直平分線；中垂線	kab txiav nruab nrab rov ntsug
perpendicular lines	مستقيمات متعامدة	垂直线	垂直線	cov kab raws seem rov ntsug
pi	النسبة التقريبية	pi（圆周率）	pi（圓周率）	qhov deb hauv lub plawv mus rau nraum lub ntug ntawm lub voj voog uas siv 3.14
pictograph	رسم بياني صوري	象形图	象形圖	txoj kev teev duab los cim ua lus los yog zauv
pie graph	رسم بياني مستدير	圆形图；饼图	圓形圖；圓瓣圖；餅圖	daim duab kos faib lub voj voog
place value	مرتبة العدد (آحاد أو عشرات أو مئات)	位值	位值	qhov chaw rau nqi rau tus zauv
plane	مستو	平面	平面	plag tiaj
plane figure	شكل مستو	平面图形	平面圖形	ib daim plag tiaj
plus	زائد / موجب	加；加号	加；加號	ntxiv, ntau dua
point	نقطة / فاصلة عشرية	点	點	tee, taw

KOREAN	SPANISH	TAGALOG	URDŪ	VIETNAMESE
평행선	líneas paralelas	mga magkahilerang guhit	متوازی خطوط	các đường thẳng song song
평행사변형	paralelogramo	paralelogramo	متوازی الاضلاع	hình bình hành
괄호	paréntesis	mga panaklong	خطوط وحدانی	dấu ngoặc đơn
부분곱	producto parcial	parsyal na produkto	جزوی مصنوع	sản phẩm chưa hoàn chỉnh, bán thành phẩm
형식	patrón	patern	انداز	khuôn mẫu, qui luật, mô hình
오각형	pentágono	pentagon	مخمّس	hình ngũ giác
백분율	por ciento	porsyento	فیصد	phần trăm
완전제곱	cuadrado perfecto	parisukat ganap	مربع کامل	bình phương chính xác
둘레	perímetro	perimetro	محیط	chu vi
순열	permutación	permutasyon	تبادل	sự hoán vị, phép hoán vị
수직	perpendicular	patayo	عمود	đường vuông góc, đường trực giao
수직이등분선	bisector mediatriz perpendicular	patayong panghati	عمودی تنصیف	đường phân giác vuông góc
수직선	líneas perpendiculares	mga patayong guhit	عمودی خطوط	các đường trực giao
파이	pi	pi	پائی	pi, bằng 3.14159
그림 그래프	pictograma	piktograpo	تصویری نشان	chữ tượng hình
파이 그래프	gráfica circular	pi na talangguhit	پائی گراف	biểu đồ hình bánh
자릿수	valor posicional	ugar na halaga	قدر مقام	trị số theo vị trí
평면	plano	patag	مسطح	mặt phẳng
평면도형	figura plana	patag na pigura	مستوی تصویر	hình phẳng
+	más	idagdag	جوڑ	số dương, cộng với (số)
점	punto	tuldok	نقطه	điểm

Mathematics Vocabulary in Nine Languages

ENGLISH	ARABIC	CHINESE SIMPLIFIED	CHINESE TRADITIONAL	HMONG
polygon	مضلع / متعدد الأضلاع	多边形	多邊形	lub xwm muaj ntau tshaj peb sab ncaj ncaj
polyhedron	شكل متعدد الأوجه	多面体	多面體	lub xwm ntom nti uas muaj ntau ntau sab
population	تعداد	总体；物件总体；全域；人口总数；人口	總體；物件總體；全域；人口總數；人口	tag nrho ib yam dab tsi/haiv neeg
positive number	عدد موجب	正数	正數	zauv positive, zauv zoo
pound	رطل / جنيه	磅；英镑；镑	磅；英鎊；鎊	ntsuas qhov nyhav
power	أس / قوة	幂；乘方；功率；检定力	冪；乘方；功率；檢定力	npaug zog, lub zog
prediction	تنبؤ	预测；预报	預測；預報	kwv yees
prime factorization	التحليل إلى العوامل الأساسية / القواسم الأولية	素因式分解；质因子分解；质数因子分解法	素因式分解；質因子分解；質數因子分解法	txoj kev nsuas txo cov zauv kom los txog cov zauv me/qis tshaj plaws
prime number	عدد أولي	素数；质数	素數；質數	cov zauv me/qis tshaj plaws uas tsis yog tawm ntawm lwm ob tug zauv los, tiam sis yog tawm ntawm 1 thiab tus zauv kheej xwb
principal	رئيسي / أساسي	主要的；本金	主要的；本金	tus nqi tiv, tus siab tshaj plaws, lub ntsiab
prism	منشور	棱柱（体）；角柱（体）	稜柱（體）；角柱（體）	lub xwm ntom nti uas muaj cov sab rov tav toj mus ib seem thiab rov ntsug mus ib seem
probability	الاحتمال	概率	概率	feem kws yees
product	حاصل	乘积；积	乘積；積	khun tawm
proper fraction	كسر حقيقي	真分数	真分數	nqe zauv zoo uas tus zauv saum toj me dua tus hauv qab
property	خاصية	性质	性質	chaw, khoom
proportion	نسبة / تناسب	比例	比例	sib piv, luaj li cas, npaum li cas
protractor	منقلة	量角器	量角器	tus ciaj siv ntsuas ces kaum thiab teev kev ntsuas

KOREAN	SPANISH	TAGALOG	URDŪ	VIETNAMESE
다각형	polígono	poligono	كثير الاضلاع	hình đa giác
다면체	poliedro	polyhedron	كثير السطوح	khối đa diện
모집단	población	populasyon	آبادی	dân số, mật độ dân số
양수	número positivo	positibong bilang	مثبت عدد	số dương
파운드	libra	libra	پاؤنڈ	pao, pound
거듭제곱	potencia	lakas	طاقت	lũy thừa
예측	predicción	prediksyon	پیش گوئی	dự báo, ước tính (danh từ)
소인수분해	factorización prima	prime factorization	اولین عدد کو جزو ضربی میں بدلنا	tìm thừa số nguyên tố
소수	número primo	gansal na bilang	اولین عدد	số nguyên tố
주	capital	pangunahin	اصول	chính
각기둥	prisma	prisma	منشور	hình lăng trụ
확률	probabilidad	probabilidad	امکان	xác suất
곱	producto	produkto	مصنوع	tích số
진분수	fracción propia	tamang hating-bilang	کسر خالص	phân số thích hợp
성질	propiedad	katangian	خصوصیت	tính chất, đặc tính
비례	proporción	proporsyon	تناسب	tỷ lệ thức
각도기	transportador	protraktor	پروٹریکٹر	thước đo góc

Mathematics Vocabulary in Nine Languages

ENGLISH	ARABIC	CHINESE SIMPLIFIED	CHINESE TRADITIONAL	HMONG
pyramid	هرم / شكل هرمي	棱锥（体）；角锥（体）	棱錐（體）；角錐（體）	lub xwm ntom nti uas muaj peb sab mus sib twb saum lub ncov
Q				
quadrilateral	شكل رباعي الأضلاع	四边形	四邊形	lub xwm muaj plaub sab thiab plaub lub ces kaum
qualitative	نوعي / كيفي	定性；性质上的；质的；定性的	定性；性質上的；質的；定性的	hais txog kev zoo
quantitative	كمي / مقداري	量的；定量	量的；定量	hais txog qhov coob, ntau
quart	كوارت (ربع جالون)	夸脱（容量单位）	夸脱（容量單位）	ntsuas kua
quarter	ربع	四分之一；十五分钟；二角五分银币	四分之一；十五分鐘；二角五分銀幣	ib feem plaub
quarter hour	ربع ساعة	一刻钟	一刻鐘	kaum tsib feeb ntawm ib teev
quarter turn	ربع دورة	四分之一转	四分之一轉	tig mus ib feem plaub
quotient	ناتج القسمة	商；商式	商；商式	qhov tawm los ntawm kev sib faib
R				
radius	نصف القطر	半径	半徑	txoj kab ntsuas hauv plawv voj voog rau nraum ntug
range	مدى / مجال / نطاق	值域；区域；范围；极差；分布域	值域；區域；範圍；極差；分佈域	qhov qib ntawm pib thiab xaus
rate	معدل	率；利率	率；利率	tus nqi, qib
ratio	نسبة	比；比率	比；比率	qhov ntsuas pes tsawg ntawm ib yam twg
rational numbers	أعداد جذرية	有理数	有理數	cov zauv tseeb
ray	شعاع	射线；辐射线；放射状线条	射線；輻射線；放射狀線條	txoj kab tshwm ntawm ib qhov chaw tuaj mus
reciprocal	معكوس / مقلوب	倒数	倒數	zoo tib yam
rectangle	مستطيل	长方形；矩形	長方形；矩形	lub xwm ob sab ntev ob sab luv
rectangular prism	منشور قائم	直角棱镜	直角棱鏡	lub xwm ntom nti muaj plaub sab ntev zoo sib xws ob tog luv zoo sib xws

KOREAN	SPANISH	TAGALOG	URDŪ	VIETNAMESE
각뿔	pirámide	piramide	ابرام	hình chóp
Q				
사변형	cuadrilátero	kwadrilateral	ذو اربعّة الاضلاع	tứ giác
정성적	cualitativo	kalitatibo	مابینتی	định tính, chất lượng
정량적	cuantitativo	kanitatibo	کَمّیتی	định lượng
쿼트	cuarto de galón	galon	ظرف	lít Anh
4분의 1	cuarto	ikaapat	چوتہائی	một phần tư, đồng 25 xu
25분	cuarto de hora	ikaapat sa isang oras	چوتہائی گھنٹہ	một phần tư giờ (mười lăm phút)
4분의 1 회전	cuarto de giro	ikaapat na baling turn	چوتہائی موڑ	một phần tư vòng quay
몫	cociente	kabahaginan	خارج قسمت	thương số
R				
반경, 반지름	radio	radyus	نصف قطر	bán kính
범위	intervalo	lawak	قطار	phạm vi, tầm
율	tasa	antas	شرح	tốc độ, tỷ lệ, mức
비, 율	razón	panumbasan	تناسب	tỷ lệ
유리수	números racionales	mga rational na bilang	تناسبی اعداد	các số hữu tỷ
반직선, 사선	rayo	rayo	شعاع	bán kính
역수, 상반	recíproco	katugon	معکوسی	đảo, thuận nghịch
직사각형	rectángulo	parihaba	مستطیل	hình chữ nhật
직각 프리즘	prisma rectangular	parihabang prismo	مستطیلی منشور	hình lăng trụ vuông

Mathematics Vocabulary in Nine Languages

ENGLISH	ARABIC	CHINESE SIMPLIFIED	CHINESE TRADITIONAL	HMONG
reduce	يختزل / ينقص	简化；约简；减少	簡化；約簡；減少	lov kom tsawg, kom me
reflect	يعكس	反射	反射	ua rov qab, ua kom tshwm
reflection	انعكاس / عكس	反射；反影	反射；反影	teeb kom ib sab ntawm lub plag zoo sib xws li sab twb muaj lawm
reflective symmetry	تماثل انعكاسي	反射对称；镜相对称	反射對稱；鏡相對稱	kev teeb kom ob sab zoo sib xws nkaus
regrouping	إعادة تجميع	重行组合	重行組合	kho dua tshiab kom los ua ib pawg dua
regular polygon	مضلع منتظم	正多边形	正多邊形	lub xwm uas tag nrho cov sab thiab cov ces kaum luaj tib yam, zoo sib xws
relative frequency table	جدول التواتر النسبي	相对频数表	相對頻數表	teeb qhia tias tshwm sim heev npaum li cas
remainder	باقي الطرح	余数；余式；剩余	餘數；餘式；剩餘	tus seem
repeating pattern	نمط متكرر	重复样型；重复图样；重复图形	重覆樣型；重覆圖樣；重覆圖形	rov muaj dua cov qauv qub
rhombus	معين	菱形	菱形	lub xwm muaj plaub sab thiab plaub lub ces kaum uas cov sab tav toj thiab rov ntsug raws seem
right	قائم / عمودي / مستقيم	右面；右边；右侧；右，右方的，右侧的；直角的	右面；右邊；右側；右，右方的，右側的；直角的	yog, sab xis
right angle	زاوية قائمة	直角	直角	lub ces kaum ntsuas muaj 90
right solid	مجسم قائم	直角立体模型	直角立體模型	lub xwm uas cov sab ntug rov ntsug tav ncaj ncaj mus tshuam cov sab ntug rov tav
right triangle	مثلث قائم الزاوية	直角三角形	直角三角形	lub xwm muaj peb lub ces kaum uas ntsuas muaj 90
Roman numerals	الأرقام الرومانية	罗马数字	羅馬數字	Cov zauv sau ua ntawv Roman
rotate	يتعاقب / يدور على محور	旋转	旋轉	sib hloo, kiv
rotation	تعاقب / دوران محوري	旋转；回转	旋轉；迴轉	txoj kev sib hloo, txoj kev kiv

KOREAN	SPANISH	TAGALOG	URDŪ	VIETNAMESE
축소, 축약	reducir	pinaliit	کم کرنا	rút gọn, giảm
반사하다	reflejar	isalamin	عکس ڈالنا	phản xạ, phản chiếu, bức xạ
반사	reflexión	pagsasalamin	عکس	phản xạ
반사 대칭	simetría de reflexión	isinalaming simetro	انعکاسی تشاکل	sự đối xứng phản xạ
재분류	reagrupamiento	igrupo ulit	دوباره گروپ بندی	tạo nhóm mới, tái gộp nhóm
정다각형	polígono regular	regular na poligono	مستقل کثیر الاضلاع	hình đa giác đều
상대도수분포표	tabla de frecuencias relativas	relative na talaan ng kadalasan	متعلقہ جدول تعدّد	bảng tần số tương quan
나머지, 잔차	residuo	natira	باقی	số dư
순환 형식	patrón que se repite	paulit-ulit na pattern	دوبرانے کا انداز	qui luật, qui luật lặp lại
마름모	rombo	rombus	معیّن	hình thoi
오른쪽	derecha	suket	درست	vuông
직각	ángulo recto	sukat na anggulo	زاویۂ قائمہ	góc vuông
직각형	sólido recto	sukat na solido	عین ٹھوس	khối vuông
직각삼각형	triángulo rectángulo	sukat na trianggulo	مثلث قائمہ	tam giác vuông
로마 숫자	números romanos	Roman numerals	رومن اعداد	số La mã
회전하다	rotar	iikot	گھومنا	luân phiên nhau, xen kẽ
회전	rotación	pag-ikot	گھماؤ	luân phiên (danh từ)

Mathematics Vocabulary in Nine Languages

ENGLISH	ARABIC	CHINESE SIMPLIFIED	CHINESE TRADITIONAL	HMONG
rotational symmetry	تماثل دوراني	回转对称	迴轉對稱	txoj kev kiv ib yam uas muaj tuav ruaj hauv lub plawv
round	مستدير / دائري	圆形；圆形的；球形的；圆筒形的；弧形的	圓形；圓形的；球形的；圓筒形的；弧形的	kheej kheej, suav mus
rounded number	عدد مُقرب	约整数；舍数；四舍五入	約整數；捨數；四捨五入	tus zauv suav lawm
row	صف	行；横列	行；橫列	kab tav toj
ruler	مسطرة	直尺	直尺	pas ntsuas zauv
S				
sales tax	ضريبة المبيعات	营业税；销售税	營業稅；銷售稅	se muas khoom
sample	عينة / نموذج	样本；样品；采样；抽样	樣本；樣品；採樣；抽樣	qauv, piv txwv
sample space	مجموعة الحلول الافتراضية	样本空间	樣本空間	chaw ua qauv
scale	مقياس / ميزان	比例尺；标度；图尺；(尺、秤等上刻划的)分度度数；标；刻度；// 尺寸；尺；尺度 等级（表）//（数学)计数法进位法；换算法	比例尺；標度；圖尺；(尺、秤等上刻劃的)分度；度數；標；刻度// 尺寸；尺；尺度；等級（表)//（數學)計數法；進位法；換算法	ciaj ntsuas nyhav
scale drawing	رسم بمقياس نسبي	按原物比例画图	按原物比例畫圖	kev ntsuas thiab kos
scale factor	عامل القياس	尺度因子；标度因子；缩放系数；缩放度	尺度因子；標度因子；縮放係數；縮放度	tus zauv siv los ntsuas thiaj kos tau
scale model	نموذج مُصغر / نموذج بياني نسبي	尺寸模型；尺度模型；按比例缩放模型	尺寸模型；尺度模型；按比例縮放模型	ntsuas kos ua qauv
scalene triangle	مثلث مختلف الأضلاع	不等边三角形；不规则三角形	不等邊三角形；不規則三角形	lub xwm muaj peb sab uas tsis muaj ob sab sib luag li
second	ثانية / ثان	第二；秒	第二；秒	qib ob, zaum ob, tus ob
sector	قطاع	扇形（面）；扇式	扇形（面）；扇式	tus pas ntsuas uas quav tau ob tog los ntsuas ces kaum
segment	قطعة دائرية / جزء	段；节	段；節	ntu txiav tawm
sequence	متتالية	序列	序列	sib law liag
set	مجموعة	集；组	集；組	teeb, tiav

KOREAN	SPANISH	TAGALOG	URDŪ	VIETNAMESE
회전 대칭	simetría de rotación	paikot na simetriya	گھماؤ دار منشور	sự đối xứng xen kẽ
반올림	redondear	bilog	گول	tròn, vòng tròn
어림수	número redondeado	rounded number	قریب قریب تعداد	số được làm tròn
행	fila	hanay	قطار	hàng, dãy
자	regla	panukat	رولر	thước kẻ
S				
판매세	impuesto sobre la venta	buwis sa pagbenta	سیلس ٹیکس	thuế doanh thu, thuế bán hàng
표본	muestra	sampol	نمونه	ví dụ mẫu, mẫu
표본공간	espacio muestral	sample space	نمونے کی جگہ	khoảng cách mẫu
스케일	escala	iskala	اسکیل	sự chia độ, thang chia độ, thang điểm, tỷ lệ
축척도, 확대/축소도	dibujo a escala	guhit sa iskala	اسکیل ڈرائنگ	bản vẽ theo kích thước tỷ lệ
눈금 인자	factor de escala	paktora ng iskala	اسکیل جزو ضربی	yếu tố tỷ lệ
눈금 모형	modelo a escala	iskalang modelo	اسکیل ماڈل	mô hình tỷ lệ
부등변 삼각형	triángulo escaleno	scalene na trianggulo	مثلث مختلف الاضلاع	tam giác thường
초	segundo	ikalawa	دوسرا	thứ nhì, thứ hai
부채꼴	sector	sektor	پرکار	hình quạt
선분	segmento	bahagi	قطعۂ دائره	hình viên phân, hình cầu phân, đoạn
수열	secuencia	pagkakasunod-sunod	تواتر	dãy, chuỗi
집합	conjunto	pangkat	ترتیب	tập hợp, bộ

Mathematics Vocabulary in Nine Languages

ENGLISH	ARABIC	CHINESE SIMPLIFIED	CHINESE TRADITIONAL	HMONG
seventh	سابع / سُبع	第七	第七	qib xya
shape	شكل	形状	形狀	xwm zoo li cas
short division	القسمة المختصرة	短除法	短除法	kev faib zauv yooj yooj yim
shorter	أقصر	更短；较短；更短的；较短的	更短；較短；更短的；較短的	luv dua, qis dua
shortest	الأقصر	最短；最短的	最短；最短的	luv heev tshaj, qis heev tshaj
side	ضلع / طرف / جانب	边；侧	邊；側	sab
similar	متشابه / متماثل	相似	相似	zoo sib xws
simple interest	فائدة بسيطة (غير مركبة)	单利；单利息	單利；單利息	pauj laum them rau tib tug nqi
simplest form	أبسط الأشكال	最简式；最简形	最簡式；最簡形	faib kom tau cov zauv me tshaj plaws
sixth	سادس / سُدس	第六	第六	qib rau
size	الحجم	尺寸；大小	尺寸；大小	luaj li cas
slide	انزلاق / منزلق	滑面；滑动	滑面；滑動	ntog lam, ua zawv zawg
small	صغير	小；小的	小；小的	me
smaller	أصغر	更小；较小；更小的；较小的	更小；較小；更小的；較小的	me dua
smallest	الأصغر	最小；最小的	最小；最小的	me heev tshaj
solid	مجسم / مصمت	立体；固体	立體；固體	ntom nti tsis khoob
sort	نوع / صنف	种类；类别；分类	種類；類別；分類	xaiv, faib
sphere	كرة / جسم كروي	球形；球面	球形；球面	lub xwm kheej kheej khoob
square	شكل مربع / تربيع العدد	平方；正方形	平方；正方形	lub xwm muaj plaub sab ntug sib luag zos
square centimeter	سنتيمتر مربع	平方公分；平方厘米	平方公分；平方釐米	ntsuas plaub sab raws xeestismev
square inch	بوصة مربعة	平方英寸	平方英寸	ntsuas plaub sab raws nti
square number	تربيع العدد	平方数	平方數；正方形數	ob npaug tus zauv
square root	الجذر التربيعي	平方根；二次根	平方根；二次根	tus zauv faib los ntawm lwm tus zauv
statistics	الإحصاء / إحصائيات	统计数字；统计数据；统计表	統計數字；統計資料；統計表	kev soj ntsuam tau zoo li cas
stem-and-leaf plot	مخطط الأصل والفروع البياني	茎叶图	莖葉圖	kos duab kav thiab nplooj teev tej kev soj ntsuam tau

KOREAN	SPANISH	TAGALOG	URDŪ	VIETNAMESE
일곱번째	séptimo	ika-pito	ساتواں	thứ bảy
모양	forma	hugis	شکل	hình dạng, hình
단제법	división corta	maikling paghahati	مختصر تقسیم	phép chia ngắn
더 짧은	más corto	mas maikli	مختصر تر	ngắn hơn
가장 짧은	el más corto	pinakamaikli	مختصر ترین	ngắn nhất
변	lado	tabi	سمت	cạnh
닮음	semejante	kapareho	ایک جیسا	đồng dạng, tương tự, giống nhau
단리	interés simple	pinakapayak na interes	سود مفرد	lãi đơn
약분	forma más simple	pinakapayak na anyo	ساده ترین شکل	dạng đơn giản nhất
여섯번째	sexto	ika-anim	چھٹا	thứ sáu
크기	tamaño	laki	سائز	cỡ, kích thước, độ lớn
슬라이드	deslizar	slide	سلائڈ	trượt (danh từ), mặt nghiêng
작은	pequeño	maliit	چھوٹا	bé, nhỏ
더 작은	más pequeño	mas maliit	نسبتا چھوٹا	bé hơn, nhỏ hơn
가장 작은	el más pequeño	pinakamaliit	سب سے چھوٹا	bé nhất, nhỏ nhất
입체	sólido	solido	ٹھوس	hình khối, hình ba chiều
분류	clasificar	hanapin	ترتیب دینا	thứ, hạng, lựa chọn, sắp xếp, phân loại
구	esfera	globo	کرہ، دائرہ	hình cầu
정사각형, 제곱	cuadrado	parisukat	مربع	vuông, vuông góc
제곱 센티미터	centímetro cuadrado	parisukat na sentimetro	مربع سنٹی میٹر	xen-ti-mét vuông
제곱 인치	pulgada cuadrada	parisukat na pulgada	مربع انچ	insơ vuông
제곱수	número cuadrado	parisukat na bilang	مربع عدد	số bình phương
제곱근	raíz cuadrada	square root	جذر	căn bậc hai
통계	estadística	estadistika	شماریات	số liệu thống kê
줄기잎 그림	diagrama de tallo y hojas	stem-and-leaf plot	اسٹیم اور لیف پلاٹ	biểu đồ hình cây

Mathematics Vocabulary in Nine Languages

ENGLISH	ARABIC	CHINESE SIMPLIFIED	CHINESE TRADITIONAL	HMONG
straight angle	زاوية مستقيمة	平角	平角	ob lub ces kaum ntsuas muaj 90 yog ib lub ces kaum ntseg
subtract	يطرح	减；减去	減；減去	rho, tshem tawm
subtraction	الطرح	减法	減法	kev rho tawm
subtrahend	العدد المطروح	减数	減數	tus zauv ob ntawm nqe zauv uas yog tus raug muab rho tawm
sum	جمع / مجموع / حاصل جمع	和	和	sib ntxiv tawm
supplementary angles	زاويتان متكاملتان	补角	補角	ob lub ces kaum uas sib ntxiv los muaj 180
surface area	مساحة السطح	表面面积；曲面面积	表面面積；曲面面積	cov sab ntug sib ntxiv
survey	مسح	测量（土地）；勘查	測量（土地）；勘查	soj ntsuam, tshawb xyuas
symbol	رمز	符号；记号	符號；記號	cim
symmetrical	متماثل / متناظر	对称的	對稱的	ob yam zoo tib yam
symmetry	تماثل / تناظر	对称；对称性	對稱；對稱性	ob sab zoo tib yam
T				
table	جدول / قائمة	表；数表	表；數表	lub rooj, ntawv teev
take away	يطرح / يقتطع	减去	減去	tshem tawm
taller	أطول	更高；较高；更高的；较高的	更高；較高；更高的；較高的	siab dua
tallest	الأطول	最高；最高的	最高；最高的	siab heev tshaj
tally	يحسب / يحصي / سجل	计数	計數	cim qhia tias muaj pes tsawg
temperature	درجة الحرارة	温度	溫度	huab cua, kub txias
ten thousands	عشرة آلاف	万	萬	kaum phav
tens	عشرات	十	十	kaum
tenth	عاشر / عُشر / جزء من العشرة	第十	第十	qib kaum
term	حد / طرف (في معادلة)	项	項	lo lus, nqe lus
tessellation	اصطفاف فسيفسائي	密铺；铺嵌；嵌砌	密鋪；鋪嵌；嵌砌	kev teeb qauv
theoretical probability	الاحتمالية النظرية	理论概率	理論概率	feem uas xav tias yuav tshwm sim dua
thermometer	ترمومتر / مقياس الحرارة	温度计；体温表	溫度計；體溫表	cia ntsuas kub thiab txias
third	ثالث / ثُلث	第三	第三	qib peb

KOREAN	SPANISH	TAGALOG	URDŪ	VIETNAMESE
평각	ángulo recto	tuwid na anggulo	زاویہ مستقیم	góc bẹt
빼다	restar	bawasan	گھٹانا	trừ
뺄셈	resta	pagbabawas	گھٹاؤ	phép trừ
감수	sustraendo	ang babawasan	عدد مفروق	số bị trừ
합	suma	kabuuan	کل مقدار	tổng
보각	ángulo suplementarios	suplementaryong anggulo	تکملی زاویہ	các góc phụ
곡면넓이	área superficial	lawak ng ibabaw	سطح کا رقبہ	diện tích bề mặt
조사	encuesta	pagsisiyasat	سروے	sự khảo sát
기호	símbolo	simbolo	علامت	ký hiệu, biểu tượng
대칭의	simétrico	simetrikal	تشاکلی	đối xứng, cân đối
대칭	simetría	simetriya	تشاکل	đối xứng
T				
표	tabla	talaan	جدول	bảng, biểu
빼다, 삭제하다	restar	alisin	لے جانا	lấy đi, rút đi
키가 더 큰, 더 높은	más alto	mas mataas	نسبتا لمبا	cao hơn
키가 가장 큰, 가장 높은	el más alto	pinakamataas	سب سے لمبا	cao nhất
계정, 계산	marca de conteo	tayahin	ٹیلی	kiểm, đếm, số điểm, số tính toán
온도	temperatura	temperatura	درجۂ حرارت	nhiệt độ
10,000	decenas de miles	sampung libo	دس ہزار	hàng chục ngàn
십자리의 수	decenas	sampu	دہائی	hàng chục
열번째	décima	ikasampu	دسواں	thứ mười
항	término	termino	میعاد	số hạng
쪽 맞추기	mosaico	tessellation	پچی کاری	sự khảm, sự lát đá hoa nhiều màu
이론적 확률	probabilidad teórica	theoretical probability	نظری امکان	xác suất về mặt lý thuyết
온도계	termómetro	termometro	تھرما میٹر	nhiệt kế, nhiệt biểu kế
세번째	tercio	ikatatlo	تیسرا	thứ ba

Mathematics Vocabulary in Nine Languages

ENGLISH	ARABIC	CHINESE SIMPLIFIED	CHINESE TRADITIONAL	HMONG
thousands	آلاف	千	千	phav
thousandth	الألف / جزء من الألف	第一千（的）； 千分之一（的）	第一千（的）； 千分之一（的）	qib phav
tick mark	علامة صغيرة / يشر بعلامة صغيرة	刻度；验证标志	刻度；驗證標誌	kos cim
time	وقت / زمن	时间	時間	sij hawm
ton	طن	吨	噸	nyhav ob phav phaus
total	مجموع / حاصل جمع / إجمالي / كلي	总数	總數	tag nrho, tawm
transformation	تحويل	变换	變換	txoj kev muab teeb kos
translation	ترجمة / نقل	平移	平移	txoj kev muab los yog txav sib npaug zos
transversal	قاطع مستعرض	截线；贯线； 横向的；横切的； 横断的；截断的； 截线的	截線；貫線； 橫向的；橫切的； 橫斷的；截斷的； 截線的	txoj kab uas tshuam lwm cov kab
trapezium	الشكل المنحرف	梯形	梯形	lub xwm muaj plaub sab uas cov sab tsis raws seem ncaj sib xws
trapezoid	شبه منحرف	梯形的	梯形的	lub xwm muaj plaub sab uas ob sab raws seem ncaj sib xws hos ob sab tsis ncaj raws seem
tree diagram	رسم تخطيطي شجري	树形图	樹形圖	daim duab kos li tso ntoo teev cov soj ntsuam tau
triangle	مثلث	三角形	三角形	lub xwm peb ces kaum
triangular numbers	الأعداد الثلاثية	三角形数	三角形數	cov zauv uas ntsuas muaj peb kab thiab peb tee thooj txhij
triangular prism	المنشور الثلاثي	三棱柱；三角柱； 三棱镜	三棱柱；三角柱； 三棱鏡	lub xwm ntom nti uas lub qab muaj peb ces kaum
turn	دورة / دوران	转；转动；旋转； 翻转	轉；轉動；旋轉； 翻轉	kiv, tig
twelfth	ثاني عشر / جزء من اثني عشر	第十二	第十二	qib kaum ob

KOREAN	SPANISH	TAGALOG	URDŪ	VIETNAMESE
천자리의 수	miles	libo	بزاروں	hàng ngàn
천번째	milésima	isa-isang libo	بزارواں	một phần ngàn
체크 표시	tilde	tik mark	ٹک مارک	dấu kiểm
시간	hora	oras	وقت	thời gian, giờ
톤	tonelada	tonelada	ٹن	tấn
합계	total	total	کل	tính tổng, tổng cộng, tổng
변환	transformación	pagbabago	تحویل مساوات	phép biến đổi
평행이동	traslación	pagsasalin	ترجمہ	sự tịnh tiến
횡단선	transversal	nakahalang	خط قاطع	đường hoành, đường ngang
부등변 사각형	trapezoide	trapezium	منحرف	hình thang, hình tứ giác
사다리꼴	trapecio	trapesoyde	مربع منحرف نما	hình thang, hình tứ giác
수형도	diagrama de árbol	tree diagram	شجری خطیہ	sơ đồ hình cây
삼각형	triángulo	trianggulo	مثلث	tam giác
삼각수	números triangulares	mga trianggulong bilang	مثلث نما اعداد	các chữ số có thể tạo thành tam giác đều
삼각기둥	prisma triangular	trianggulo na prisma	مثلث نما منشور	hình lăng trụ tam giác
회전	giro	baling	موڑ	quay, đổi, vòng
열두번째	decimosegunda	ikalabingdalawa	باربواں	thứ mười hai

Mathematics Vocabulary in Nine Languages

ENGLISH	ARABIC	CHINESE SIMPLIFIED	CHINESE TRADITIONAL	HMONG
U				
under	سفلي / أقل / أدنى / تحت	在……之下；在表面之下；（年龄、时间、价格、数量等）在……以下；低于；未满	在……之下；在表面之下；（年齡、時間、價格、數量等）在……以下；低於；未滿	hauv qab
unit	وحدة	单位	單位	ib yam
unit multiplier	مضاعف الوحدة	单元乘法器	單元乘法器	tus zauv faib uas cim 1 vim nws yog qhov ntsuas tau los ntawm ob yam sib npaug zos
unknown	مجهول / قيمة مجهولة	未知数；未知量	未知數；未知量	tsis paub
unlikely	بعيد الاحتمال	未必可能的	未必可能的	tsis muaj feem
U.S. Customary System	نظام المقاييس الأمريكي	美制计量体系；美国计量体系	美製度量衡體系；美國度量體系	Teb Chaws Asmeskas Txoj Kev Ntsuas qhov nyhav, qhov puv, qhov ntev
V				
variable	متغير / كمية متغيرة	变项；变量；元；变元；变数	變項；變量；元；變元；變數	hloov mus hloov los
Venn diagram	مُخطط "فن": لبيان العلاقة بين المجموعات باستخدام الأشكال	温氏图；范氏图	溫氏圖；范氏圖	txoj kev teeb cov zauv ntsuas los xyuas qhov sib txawv ntawm txhua yam
vertex	رأس	顶（点）	頂（點）	lub ces kaum
vertical	رأسي / عمودي	垂直；铅垂	垂直；鉛垂	rov ntsug
vertical axis	محور عمودي	垂直轴	垂直軸	txoj kab kos rov ntsug ntawm nruab nrab ib yam
vertical line	خط رأسي	纵线；垂直线；铅垂	縱線；垂直線；鉛垂	txoj kab rov ntsug
volume	حجم	体积	體積	qhov puv
W				
weekday	يوم عمل من أيام الأسبوع	工作日；星期一至星期五中的某一天	工作日；週一至週五中的某一天	cov hnub khwv
weekend	عطلة نهاية الأسبوع	周末	週末	cov hnub so
weight	وزن	重量；重力	重量；重力	qhov nyhav

KOREAN	SPANISH	TAGALOG	URDŪ	VIETNAMESE
U				
이하, 미만	debajo	Sa ilalim	تحت	dưới
단위, 단원	unidad	yunit	اکائی	đơn vị
단위 승수	factor de conversión	yunit na pagpaparami	اکائی کا ضرب کننده	số nhân đơn vị
미지수	desconocido	di-alam	نا معلوم	ẩn số
확률이 없는	poco probable	maaaring di-mangyari	غیر امکانی	không chắc đúng, không có khả năng, không chắc sẽ
미국 도량형 제도	Sistema usual de EE.UU.	U.S. Customary System	امریکی مروّجہ نظام	Hệ Thống Đơn Vị Đo Lường Hoa Kỳ
V				
문자(변수)	variable	variable	قابل تغیّر	biến số
벤다이어그램	diagrama de Venn	Venn diagram	وین خطیہ	biểu đồ Venn
꼭지점	vértice	taluktok	راس	đỉnh
수직의	vertical	patayo	عمودی	thẳng (tính từ)
수직축	eje vertical	patayong axis	عمودی محور	trục thẳng
수직선	línea vertical	patayong guhit	عمودی خط	đường thẳng
부피	volumen	bulto	حجم	thể tích, dung tích, dung lượng
W				
주중	entre semana	araw ng linggo	ہفتے کا دن	ngày thường, ngày trong tuần
주말	fin de semana	katapusan ng linggo	اواخر ہفتہ	cuối tuần, ngày cuối tuần
무게, 가중치	peso	timbang	وزن	trọng lượng

Mathematics Vocabulary in Nine Languages

ENGLISH	ARABIC	CHINESE SIMPLIFIED	CHINESE TRADITIONAL	HMONG
whole	كامل / تام / كل / وحدة كاملة	整体；整个	整體；整個	kheej, tag nrho
whole numbers	الأعداد الصحيحة	整数	整數	cov zauv ib tug zus
width	العرض	宽度；阔度	寬度；闊度	qhov dav
X				
x-axis	المحور السيني / محور السينات	x 轴	x 軸	kab ntsug x
Y				
yard	ياردة	码	碼	yas npab
y-axis	المحور الصادي / محور الصادات	y 轴	y 軸	kab ntsug y
Z				
zero	صفر	零	零	tsis muaj dab tsi, 0
Zero Property of Multiplication	الخاصية الصفرية للضرب	乘法的零乘性质	乘法的零乘性質	Txoj kev siv 0 los khun zauv

KOREAN	SPANISH	TAGALOG	URDŪ	VIETNAMESE
전체	entero	buo	سالم	tổng, toàn bộ, nguyên
범자연수	número enteros	mga buong bilang	عدد سالم	các số nguyên
폭, 너비	ancho	lapad	عرض	bề rộng, chiều rộng
X				
x축	eje x	x-axis	ایکس محور	trục hoành, trục x
Y				
야드	yarda	yarda	گز	yard
y축	eje y	y-axis	وائی محور	trục tung
Z				
0	cero	sero	صفر	không, số không
곱셈의 0 법칙	Propiedad del cero en la multiplicación	Zero Property of Multiplication	ضرب کی صفر خصوصیت	Tính Chất Bằng Không của Phép Nhân

Spanish and Mathematics

Prefixes and Suffixes

English and Spanish share some basic linguistic characteristics, such as using word parts like prefixes and suffixes and changing verb forms. The chart below provides some helpful information about prefixes and suffixes that serve similar functions in English and Spanish. Note that the example words are not intended to be cognates, but words that illustrate the similar meaning of the word parts.

Prefixes

ENGLISH WORD PART OR PARTS	ENGLISH EXAMPLE WORDS	SPANISH WORD PART OR PARTS	SPANISH EXAMPLE WORDS	WORD PART PURPOSE
un-, non-, in-, dis-	unhappy nonstop incorrect dislike	*in-, des-/dis-* no plus the verb sin plus the noun or verb	infeliz, incorrecto desconocido disparejo no gustar sin parar	Means "not"
re-	redo	*re-*	rehacer	Means "again"
pre-	preteen	*pre-*	preescolar	Means "before"

Suffixes

ENGLISH WORD PART OR PARTS	ENGLISH EXAMPLE WORDS	SPANISH WORD PART OR PARTS	SPANISH EXAMPLE WORDS	WORD PART PURPOSE
-ful	powerful	*-oso/a*	poderoso/a	Means "with"; turns a noun into an adjective
-able	readable likeable	*-ible* *-able*	legible agradable	Turns a verb into an adjective
-less	fearless careless	sin plus the noun prefix *des-*	sin miedo descuidado	Means "without"; turns a noun into an adjective
-ness	happiness	*-idad*	felicidad	Turns an adjective into a noun
-ion/-tion, -ment	reaction payment amazement	*-ción/-sión* verb stem + *-o*	reacción conclusión pago asombro	Turns a verb into a noun
-ly	quickly	*-mente*	rápidamente	Turns an adjective into an adverb

Spanish Cognates for Mathematics Vocabulary

COGNATES are words that have the same root or origin; that is, they are derived from the same word or language. Cognates can be in the same language or different languages. For example, two English words may be cognates, but an English word and a Spanish word may also be cognates.

A large number of English words (perhaps 30–40%) have similar words in Spanish. English-Spanish cognates are often similar in meaning and spelling, and have relatively close pronunciations. For Spanish-speaking students, the knowledge of cognates can help them to learn English more easily and to recognize the mathematical vocabulary they encounter. Being aware of Spanish mathematical cognates can help both teachers and students communicate more effectively within the mathematics classroom.

Suffixes for Cognates

Some Spanish cognates are spelled exactly like the English words; for example, decimal. Most, however, have a change in the suffix. Below are some common suffix changes between English and Spanish, with sample math vocabulary terms. Note that in Spanish, the accented syllable gets the most emphasis when spoken. A comprehensive list of English-Spanish cognates for Mathematics follows.

Samples of English-Spanish Math Terms			
	SUFFIX CHANGE	**ENGLISH**	**SPANISH**
Nouns	-tion → ción	multiplication	multiplicación
	-tion → xión	reflection	reflexión
	-ty → -dad	property	propiedad
		identity	identidad
	add -o	pentagon	pentágono
		gram	gramo
	change to -o	rectangle	rectángulo
	-ter → -tro	liter	litro
		perimeter	perímetro
	add -e	exponent	exponente
	add -a	median	mediana
	change to -a	symmetry	simetría
Adjectives	add -e	congruent	congruente
	change to -a	associative	asociativa
	change to -o	negative	negativo
Verbs	-e → -ar	estimate	estimar
	-e → -ir	divide	dividir
	add -ir	invert	invertir
	change to -ar	bisect	bisecar

Tips for Teaching with Cognates

BEFORE THE LESSON. Preview the math vocabulary that will be introduced in the day's lesson and review any previously-taught math terms that will be used today. Mention any math vocabulary that also has a Spanish cognate. Ask an EL student to pronounce the Spanish term.

DURING WHOLE-CLASS INSTRUCTION. As you teach a mathematical concept, ask Spanish-speaking students to raise their hand if they hear a cognate. Briefly discuss the Spanish cognate and its English counterpart, especially to compare their pronunciations.

IN SMALL-GROUP OR INDIVIDUAL WORK. As students work on problems and activities, have them keep a list of all cognates they encounter. Have them write the English term in one column and its Spanish cognate in another column.

WORD WALL. To reinforce frequently-used math vocabulary, you can create (or have students create) a word wall of English and Spanish math cognates.

Mathematical Cognates in English and Spanish

ENGLISH	SPANISH
A	
adjacent	adyacente
algebra	álgebra
algorithm	algoritmo
angle	ángulo
approximation	aproximación
area	área
arithmetic	aritmética
associative	asociativa
B	
balance	balanza
base	base
bisect	bisecar
C	
calculator	calculadora
calendar	calendario
capacity	capacidad
cardinal	cardinal
Celsius	Celsius
center	centro
centigrade	centrígrado
centimeter	centímetro
circle	círculo

ENGLISH	SPANISH
C continued	
circumference	circunferencia
column	columna
combination	combinación
common	común
commutative	conmutativa
compare	comparar
comparison	comparación
compass	compás
compatible	compatible
complement	complemento
cone	cono
congruent	congruente
coordinate	coordenada
count	contar
cube	cubo
cubic	cúbica
cylinder	cilindro
D	
data	datos
decade	década
decimal	decimal
decimeter	decímetro

ENGLISH	SPANISH
D continued	
denominador	denominador
diagram	diagrama
diameter	diámetro
difference	diferencia
digit	dígito
digital	digital
dimension	dimensión
direction	dirección
distance	distancia
distributive	distributiva
divide	dividir
dividend	dividendo
divisibility	divisibilidad
divisible	divisible
division	división
divisor	divisor
dollar	dólar
doubles	dobles
E	
element	elemento
ellipse	elipse
equal	igual
equation	ecuación
equiangular	equiangular
equilateral	equilátero
equivalent	equivalente
estimate	estimar
evaluate	evaluar
event	evento
experiment	experimento
exponent	exponente
exponential	exponencial
expression	expresión
F	
factor	factor
Fahrenheit	Fahrenheit
family	familia
Fibonacci	Fibonacci
formula	fórmula
fraction	fracción
frequency	frecuencia
function	función

ENGLISH	SPANISH
G	
gallon	galón
geoband	geobanda
geometric	geométrico
geometry	geometría
gram	gramo
graph	gráfica (noun)
graph	graficar (verb)
H	
hexagon	hexágono
histogram	histograma
horizontal	horizontal
I	
identity	identidad
infinity	infinito
impossible	imposible
improper	impropia
intersect	intersecar
inverse	inversa
invert	invertir
irrational	irracional
isósceles	isósceles
K	
kilogram	kilogramo
kilometer	kilómetro
L	
line	línea
liter	litro
M	
mass	masa
median	mediana
meter	metro
metric	métrico
milligram	miligramo
millimeter	milímetro
million	millón
minute	minuto
mode	moda
multiple	múltiplo
multiplication	multiplicación
multiply	multiplicar

ENGLISH	SPANISH
N	
negative	negativo
notation	notación
number	número
numerator	numerador
O	
oblique	oblicua
obtuse	obtuso
octagon	octágono
operation	operación
order	orden
ordinal	ordinal
origin	origen
P	
pair	par
palindrome	palíndrome
parallel	paralelas
parallelogram	paralelogramo
partial	parcial
pentagon	pentágono
perfect	perfecto
perimeter	perímetro
permutation	permutación
perpendicular	perpendicular
pi	pi
pictograph	pictografía
plane	plano
polygon	polígono
positive	positivo
prediction	predicción
prime	primo
prism	prisma
probability	probabilidad
problem	problema
product	producto
property	propiedad
proportion	proporción
pyramid	pirámide
Q	
quadrilateral	cuadrilátero
R	
radius	radio
ray	rayo

ENGLISH	SPANISH
R *continued*	
reciprocals	recíprocos
rectangle	rectángulo
rectangular	rectangular
reduce	reducir
reflect	reflejar
reflection	reflexión
regular	regular
rhombus	rombo
rotate	rotar
rotation	rotación
S	
second	segundo
sector	sector
segment	segmento
sequence	secuencia
solid	sólido
sum	suma
symmetrical	simétrico
symmetry	simetría
system	sistema
T	
table	tabla
tangram	tangramas
temperature	temperatura
thermometer	termómetro
total	total
transformation	transformación
translation	traslación
trapezoid	trapecio
triangle	triángulo
triangular	triangular
transversal	transversal
U	
unit	unidad
V	
variable	variable
Venn	Venn
vertex	vértice
vertical	vertical
volume	volumen
Y	
yard	yarda

Language Transfer Issues

Understanding Language Transfer

Students learning English come to us with myriad backgrounds, both culturally and linguistically. These backgrounds serve as marvelous resources for learning another language. For instance, all spoken languages are made up of sounds that comprise words that comprise sentences that comprise communication. We use the wealth of knowledge provided to us by our first language as a roadmap for interpreting all aspects of a second language—grammar (syntax), phonics (sounds and writing symbols), and vocabulary. This knowledge is an asset and a valuable tool in accelerating the acquisition of a second language. Just think how much harder language learning would be if a learner didn't know to look for words among the endless string of babble!

Because English language learners rely on their primary language experiences to guide their acquisition of English, transfer issues—language learning areas in which the primary language influences English production—arise. There are three types of transfer between languages.

The first is positive transfer. Cognates are an excellent example of positive transfer. If a student speaks Spanish and knows the word *teléfono*, he or she will have little trouble learning the word *telephone* in English. The two words sound similar and even have a similar spelling to a certain extent. The transfer from Spanish to English, in this case, has a positive effect. Another example of positive transfer can occur in the realm of phonics. If a student speaks Spanish and has learned that the letter *m* represents /m/, that knowledge will transfer readily to English phonics, in which the letter represents the same sound.

The second type of language transfer is zero transfer. Zero transfer occurs when something is encountered in English that is not present in the primary language. For some languages, such as Chinese, the writing system of English is a zero transfer situation. Because these languages rely on different writing systems, a student from one of these language backgrounds will not mistake the letter *j* for another sound because he or she has never encountered that writing symbol in the primary language. In a sense, the slate is clean, and while there is no assistance from the primary language as in positive transfer, there is no impediment either.

The last type of language transfer is negative transfer. In these situations, an element of the primary language conflicts with an element of English and causes difficulty in acquiring that specific element of English. A simple example is that Spanish speakers who know the word *librería* might be tempted to use their knowledge to interpret the English word *library* as a bookstore instead of as an institution that lends books to the public. In the realm of grammar, that same Spanish speaker might be tempted to place an adjective after the noun *(house big* as in *casa grande)* when constructing English sentences. And when he or she encounters the letter *j* while learning to read, the reader with Spanish language background might substitute /h/ for the English *j* sound because that is the Spanish letter-sound correspondence.

Because each primary language has unique characteristics, there are unique language transfer issues for all of the languages represented in our classrooms. This resource guide focuses on providing teachers valuable information about zero and negative language transfer issues that affect the English acquisition of our students. As part of this introduction, background information for eleven languages is provided (page 78). The first chart that follows provides grammar transfer issues for ten primary languages found among English language learners in U.S. schools (page 86). The second chart provides phonics transfer issues for seven of these primary languages (page 94).

Teachers should use this wealth of information to help them identify possible areas of difficulty for students in their classrooms during instruction and to modify expectations accordingly. For instance, it's helpful to know that Vietnamese students may not be able to produce a final *s* sound. Therefore, they may have difficulty producing sentences with accurate third-person agreement.

The phonics transfer chart is divided into two sections: sound transfer (phonology) and sound-symbol transfer (phonics). Acquiring the sound-symbol system of English phonics relies on two elements for an English language learner—first, the learner's ability to produce the English sound accurately and second, his or her ability to associate the sound produced with the correct symbol. Therefore, both the sound system and the writing system of the primary language can impact a student's English language acquisition. The sound-symbol correspondence chart includes only those languages that use the Roman alphabet because other languages have zero transfer for the entire English writing system.

Best instructional practice proceeds from the known to the unknown. Therefore, with a group of language learners with a single language background, elements of positive transfer are taught first, followed by zero transfer elements, and finally by negative transfer elements.

When encountering an element of negative transfer in a young learner's ability to produce the sounds of English, teachers often find that overt correction can raise children's anxiety, resulting in an overall negative effect for language learning. Because children who learn a second language before the age of 12 will generally acquire the sound system perfectly over time, spending instructional time on pronunciation is not necessary. Rather, modeling correct pronunciation back to students while validating their English approximations is the best course to follow.

It can also be beneficial to use knowledge about negative transfer issues to inform an instructional approach to a specific language element. For instance, when teaching the letters *b* and *v* to Spanish-speaking students (these two sounds are variants of a single phoneme, or distinctive sound, in Spanish), an approach that contrasts the English sounds and symbols of these two letters will probably yield the best results. Similarly, raising the awareness of intermediate language learners to the cause of their errors can help them learn to self-correct. *Lupita, I noticed that you said "number large." I know that's how you say it in Spanish, but we always say* large number *in English*. Metacognitive language learning strategies, those in which students are actively engaged in analyzing and improving their learning process, can accelerate language learning.

Good instruction is anchored in a well-rounded knowledge of students and their learning needs. Because teachers of English language learners cannot possibly speak all the primary languages that represent the backgrounds of each of their students, we have brought together expert language consultants for many of the primary language groups in the United States today in order to provide important information that can inform classroom instruction.

Background Information for Eleven Primary Languages

The following background information is provided to help you understand the linguistic and cultural heritage of the students in your classroom. The list features the primary languages spoken by English language learners in U.S. schools.

NORTH AMERICA

SOUTH AMERICA

ATLANTIC OCEAN

PACIFIC OCEAN

Key:

- Spanish
- Vietnamese
- Hmong (also ▨)
- Chinese Languages
- Haitian Creole
- Korean
- Khmer (Cambodian)
- Tagalog
- Russian
- Arabic
- Urdū

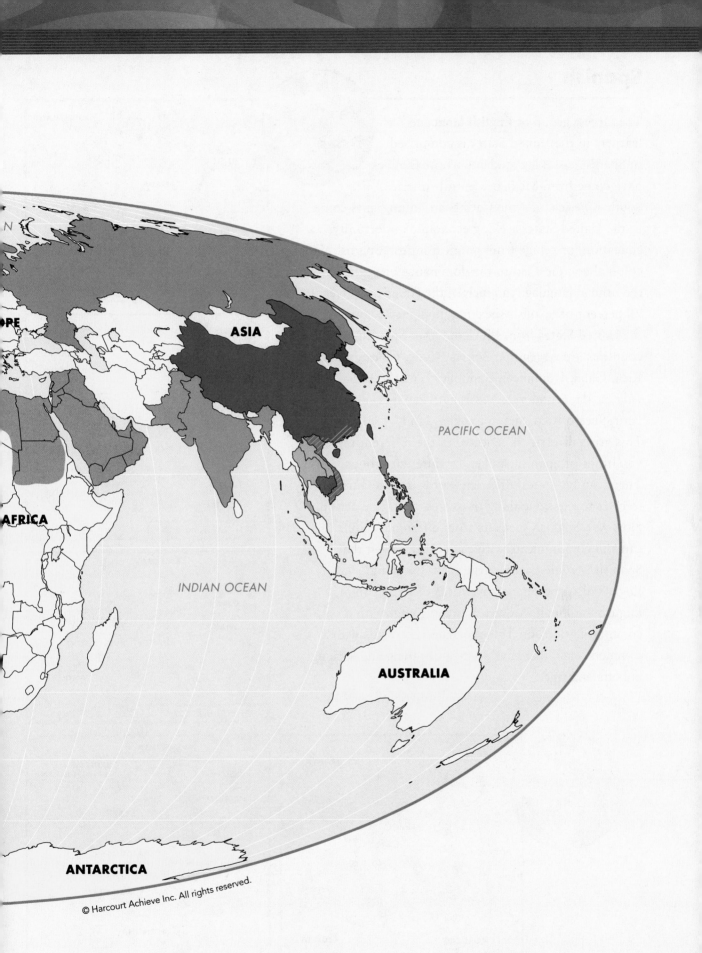

ASIA

PACIFIC OCEAN

AFRICA

INDIAN OCEAN

AUSTRALIA

ANTARCTICA

OPE

N

Spanish

The largest group of English language learners in the United States is comprised of Spanish-speaking students whose families have come from Mexico, Central America, South America, and the Caribbean. Immigrants come to the United States seeking economic opportunity, education, or refuge from political unrest. Spanish colonial conquest led to the dominance of Spanish as the official language in much of the Americas. Over 70 percent of Spanish-speaking immigrants come to the United States from Mexico. Other Spanish-speaking countries are Argentina, Bolivia, Chile, Colombia, Costa Rica, Cuba, Dominican Republic, Ecuador, El Salvador, Guatemala, Honduras, Nicaragua, Panama, Paraguay, Peru, Puerto Rico, Spain, Uruguay, and Venezuela. This great diversity is reflected in the different regional variations of Spanish spoken by different groups. There can be several different words (lexical variants) to refer to the same thing or express the same action. However, Spanish speakers from different regions can still communicate with each other. Given that Spanish is a language derived from Latin and that English also contains many words of Latin origin, English and Spanish share many cognates with a common Latin root. These cognates are words with a common origin that have a similar meaning and spelling in both languages.

NORTH AMERICA

CENTRAL AMERICA

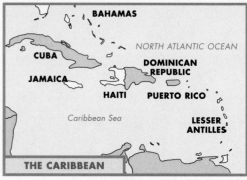

THE CARIBBEAN

SOUTH AMERICA

Saxon Math

Vietnamese

Vietnamese is one of approximately 150 languages belonging to the Austro-Asiatic family of languages. It is spoken in Vietnam, on the eastern portion of the Indo-Chinese Peninsula in Southeast Asia. The official language of Vietnam, Vietnamese, is a tonal language made up of six distinct tones. Vietnamese is written with the Roman alphabet and the use of diacritical markings to depict tones. Many Vietnamese speakers immigrated to the United States in 1975 after the end of the Vietnam War and the reunification of North and South Vietnam, and, most recently, from 1985 to 1991 through family reunification programs.

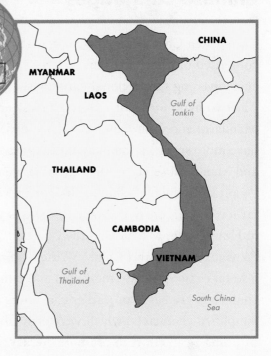

Hmong

The Hmong language is one of a group of closely related languages of Southeast Asia and Southern China often referred to as the Miao-Yao languages. It is the tonal language of an ethnic group called Hmong that is spread among several countries: China, Thailand, Laos, and Vietnam. Hmong is predominantly monosyllabic. It is made up of eight different tones, and each syllable has a particular tone associated with it. Many Hmong speakers immigrated to the United States in 1975 as refugees after the Vietnam War. Today Hmong people can be found in China, Thailand, Laos, and Vietnam as well as the United States, France, French Guiana, Argentina, Canada, Germany, and Australia.

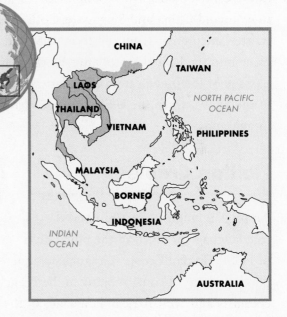

Chinese Languages

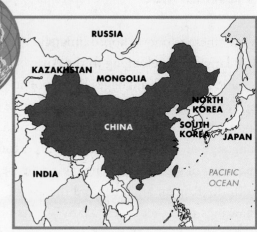

The spoken Chinese language is actually comprised of many different dialects encompassing vast regional variations. The two main forms of spoken Chinese are Mandarin and Cantonese. Mandarin dialects have more speakers than any other language in the world, and Mandarin serves as the official language of the People's Republic of China and Taiwan. Cantonese has far fewer speakers than Mandarin and is spoken primarily in Hong Kong, Macau, and the Canton (Guangdong) Province in mainland China. Written Chinese language also takes two forms: Traditional and Simplified. As their names imply, Traditional characters are based on earlier characters and are formed using more strokes than Simplified characters, which were created by the government of the People's Republic of China in an effort to promote literacy. Today, Traditional characters are still used in Taiwan, Hong Kong, Macau, and many overseas Chinese communities including those in the United States, while Simplified characters comprise the preferred writing system in mainland China and Singapore. Both Traditional and Simplified forms are typically written in columns from top to bottom and right to left. An influx of Chinese speakers came into the United States after World War II and again in the late 1960s after the passage of the Immigration and Naturalization Act of 1965. A further impetus occurred in the 1970s, when the United States offered educational opportunities to Chinese immigrants.

Haitian Creole

An official language of Haiti and the sole language of much of the population of Haiti, Haitian Creole is a language that developed out of contact between the French colonists and West African languages of the plantation workers. As a result, it contains elements of all of these languages. While much of its vocabulary is similar to French, other elements of the language, such as grammar, differ dramatically. Since 1940 three different writing systems, all based on the Roman alphabet, have been introduced for the language, resulting in widespread use of hybrid elements of each of these systems despite the Haitian government's adoption of a standard writing system in 1979. Speakers of Haitian Creole come to the United States seeking economic opportunity. Between 1981 and 1996, almost one million people left Haiti.

 Saxon Math

Korean

Korean is a non-tonal Asian language spoken in the Korean Peninsula in Northeast Asia. There are seven Korean dialects: Ham-Kyung, Pyung-Yang, Choong-Chung, Kyung-Sang, Chul-La, Che-Joo, and Central, which is spoken in Seoul and Kyung-Gui. Korean speakers can be found in both North and South Korea, China, Japan, and Russia. Many immigrated to the United States after the liberation of Korea from Japanese colonization in 1945 and again after the passage of the 1965 Immigration and Naturalization Act. Koreans continue to immigrate to the United States seeking a higher standard of living, better educational opportunities, and political stability.

Urdū

Urdū originated in South Asia as a member of the Indo-Aryan language family. Spoken by 160 million people worldwide, Urdū serves as the national language of Pakistan and one of India's 23 official languages. Urdū, along with Hindi, is a standardized form of Hindustani. Because Urdū and Hindi are extremely similar, speakers are generally understood by one another. However, the two differ in their written forms, specialized vocabularies, and socio-political connotations. Urdū is written from right to left using the Nasta'liq style of Arabic calligraphy. The Urdū-speaking population in the United States has been growing since the 1980s with the immigration of workers in the medical, engineering, and technology fields.

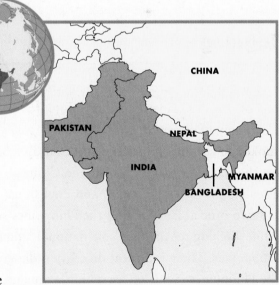

Khmer (Cambodian)

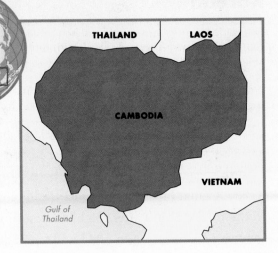

The word Khmer (pronounced kuh-MIE, rhymes with *pie*) refers to both the national language and the people of Cambodia, located in Southeast Asia. Khmer, a non-tonal language, is spoken by 90 percent of the population in Cambodia and also by many people in northeast Thailand and southern Vietnam. Cambodian Americans arrived in the United States in two waves. The first wave consisted of a small number who escaped Cambodia just before the Khmer Rouge takeover in 1975. The second wave consisted of a much larger number of refugees who fled the country after the 1979 invasion of Cambodia by Vietnam, ending the reign of the Khmer Rouge. Between 1975 and 1987, over 140,000 Cambodian refugees resettled in the United States. Refugee resettlement came to an end in the late 1980s, but Cambodian immigrants continue to arrive as Cambodian Americans sponsor family members who had been left behind.

Tagalog

Tagalog (pronounced tah-GAH-lug) is one of over 300 languages that belong to the Malayo-Polynesian family of languages spoken in the Philippines, a set of islands off the southeast coast of mainland China. Tagalog (also called Filipino) and English have been the two official languages of the Philippines since 1973, while Tagalog remains the sole national language of the Philippines. There is a great diversity of languages in the Philippines. Some of the major languages other than Tagalog include Cebuano, Ilocano, Hiligaynon, Bicol, and Waray. Tagalog speakers immigrated to the United States mainly after 1946, when their country achieved independence after being a U.S. territory for 46 years.

 Saxon Math

Russian

As a member of the Indo-European language family, the same language family as English, Russian shares some cognates with English. Cognates are words of similar meaning that sound similar between two languages. Russian is written in a left-to-right format, however, with the Cyrillic alphabet, not the Roman one. The first influx of Russian-speaking immigrants to the United States occurred during the first decades of the last century and consisted of those seeking religious and political freedom and an escape from war. A second wave of immigration to the United States from Russia occurred in the 1970s, when dissidents were exiled from the Soviet Union, many of them choosing the United States as their new country of residence. After the demise of the Soviet Union in the 1990s, more Russian immigrants have come to the United States seeking better economic opportunities and social stability.

Arabic

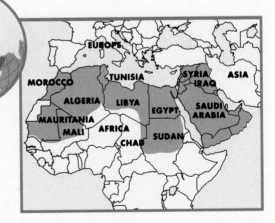

Arabic belongs to the Semitic language family. It is spoken in an area stretching from Morocco in the west to the Persian Gulf in the east. There are many varieties, including Classical Arabic, Eastern Arabic, Western Arabic, and Maltese, not all of which can be mutually understood. A Modern Standard Arabic also exists and is used in literature, education, and the media. Unlike most European languages, Arabic is written from right to left, and text starts from what we usually consider the back of a book. Its alphabet consists of 28 letters, mainly consonants, with vowels that are indicated by marks above or below the letters. Most speakers of Arabic immigrated to the United States from the nations of Syria, Lebanon, Egypt, Yemen, and Jordan. A large influx of Arabic speakers occurred after the passage of the 1965 Immigration and Naturalization Act.

Grammar Transfer Issues for Ten Languages

The following chart identifies areas in which speakers of various primary languages may have some difficulty in acquiring English grammar (syntax). The type of transfer error and its cause is outlined for each grammatical category.

Plurals and Possessives

GRAMMAR POINT	TYPE OF TRANSFER ERROR IN ENGLISH	LANGUAGE BACKGROUND	CAUSE OF TRANSFER DIFFICULTY
Plural forms	omission of plural marker –s *I have 5 book.*	Cantonese, Haitian Creole, Hmong, Khmer, Korean, Tagalog, Vietnamese	Nouns do not change form to show the plural in the primary language.
Possessive forms	avoidance of *'s* to describe possession *the children of my sister* instead of *my sister's children*	Haitian Creole, Hmong, Khmer, Spanish, Tagalog, Vietnamese	The use of a prepositional phrase to express possession reflects the only structure or a more common structure in the primary language.
	no marker for possessive forms *house my friend* instead of *my friend's house*	Haitian Creole, Khmer, Vietnamese	A noun's owner comes after the object in the primary language.
Count versus noncount nouns	use of plural forms for English noncount nouns *the furnitures* *the color of her hairs*	Haitian Creole, Russian, Spanish, Tagalog	Nouns that are count and noncount differ between English and the primary language.

Articles

	omission of article *He has job.* *His dream is to become lawyer, not teacher.*	Cantonese, Haitian Creole, Hmong, Khmer, Korean, Russian, Tagalog, Vietnamese	Articles are either lacking or the distinction between *a* and *the* is not paralleled in the primary language.
	omission of articles in certain contexts, such as to identify a profession *He is teacher.*	Spanish	The article is not used in Spanish in this context, but it is needed in English.
	overuse of articles *The honesty is the best policy.* *This food is popular in the Japan.* *I like the cats.*	Arabic, Haitian Creole, Hmong, Spanish, Tagalog	The article is used in the primary language in places where it isn't used in English.
	use of *one* for *a/an* *He is one engineer.*	Haitian Creole, Hmong, Vietnamese	Learners sometimes confuse the articles *a/an* with *one* since articles either do not exist in the primary language or serve a different function.

Pronouns

GRAMMAR POINT	TYPE OF TRANSFER ERROR IN ENGLISH	LANGUAGE BACKGROUND	CAUSE OF TRANSFER DIFFICULTY
Personal pronouns, gender	use of pronouns with inappropriate gender *He is my sister.*	Cantonese, Haitian Creole, Hmong, Khmer, Korean, Tagalog	The third person pronoun in the primary language is gender free. The same pronoun is used where English uses masculine, feminine, and neuter pronouns, resulting in confusion of pronoun forms in English.
	use of pronouns with inappropriate gender *He is my sister.*	Spanish	In Spanish, subject pronouns are dropped in everyday speech and the verb conveys third-person agreement, effectively collapsing the two pronouns and causing transfer difficulty for subject pronouns in English.
	use of inappropriate gender, particularly with neuter nouns *The house is big. She is beautiful.*	Russian, Spanish	Inanimate nouns have feminine and masculine gender in the primary language, and the gender may be carried over into English.
Personal pronoun forms	confusion of subject and object pronoun forms *Him hit me.* *I like she.* *Let we go.*	Cantonese, Hmong, Khmer	The same pronoun form is used for *he/him*, *she/her*, and in some primary languages for *I/me* and *we/us*.
	use of incorrect number for pronouns *I saw many yellow flowers. It was pretty.*	Cantonese, Korean	There is no number agreement in the primary language.
	omission of subject pronouns *Michael isn't here. Is in school.*	Korean, Russian, Spanish	Subject pronouns may be dropped in the primary language and the verb ending supplies information on number and/or gender.
	omission of object pronouns *That man is very rude, so nobody likes.*	Korean, Vietnamese	Direct objects are frequently dropped in the primary language.
	omission of pronouns in clauses *If not have jobs, they will not have food.*	Cantonese, Vietnamese	A subordinate clause at the beginning of a sentence does not require a subject in the primary language.
	use of pronouns with subject nouns *This car it runs very fast.* *Your friend he seems so nice.* *My parents they live in Vietnam.*	Hmong, Spanish, Vietnamese	This type of redundant structure reflects the popular "topic-comment" approach used in the primary language: the speaker mentions a topic and then makes a comment on it.

GRAMMAR POINT	TYPE OF TRANSFER ERROR IN ENGLISH	LANGUAGE BACKGROUND	CAUSE OF TRANSFER DIFFICULTY
	avoidance of pronouns by repetition of nouns *Sara visits her grandfather every Sunday, and Sara makes a meal.*	Korean, Vietnamese	It is common in the primary language to repeat nouns rather than to use pronouns.
Pronoun *one*	omission of the pronoun *one* *I saw two nice cars, and I like the small.*	Russian, Spanish, Tagalog	Adjectives can be used on their own in the primary language, whereas English often requires a noun or *one*.
Possessive forms	confusion of possessive forms *The book is my.*	Cantonese, Hmong, Vietnamese	Cantonese and Hmong speakers tend to omit final *n*, creating confusion between *my* and *mine*.

Adjectives

GRAMMAR POINT	TYPE OF TRANSFER ERROR IN ENGLISH	LANGUAGE BACKGROUND	CAUSE OF TRANSFER DIFFICULTY
	position of adjectives after nouns *I read a book interesting.*	Haitian Creole, Hmong, Khmer, Spanish, Vietnamese	Adjectives commonly come after nouns in the primary language.
	position of adjectives before certain pronouns *This is interesting something.*	Cantonese, Korean	Adjectives always come before words they modify in the primary language.
Comparison	omission of markers for comparison *She is smart than me.*	Khmer	Since there are no suffixes or inflections in Khmer, the tendency is to omit them in English.
	avoidance of *-er* and *-est* endings *I am more old than my brother.*	Hmong, Khmer, Korean, Spanish	Comparative and superlative are usually formed with separate words in the primary language, the equivalent of *more* and *most* in English.
Confusion of *-ing* and *-ed* forms	confusion of *-ing* and *-ed* forms *The movie was bored.* *I am very interesting in sports.*	Cantonese, Khmer, Korean, Spanish	The adjective forms in the primary language that correspond to the ones in English do not have active and passive meanings. In Korean, for many adjectives, the same form is used for both active and passive meanings, such as *boring* versus *bored*.

Verbs and Tenses

GRAMMAR POINT	TYPE OF TRANSFER ERROR IN ENGLISH	LANGUAGE BACKGROUND	CAUSE OF TRANSFER DIFFICULTY
Present tense	omission of *s* in present tense, third person agreement *She go to school every day.*	Cantonese, Haitian Creole, Hmong, Khmer, Korean, Tagalog, Vietnamese	There is no subject-verb agreement in the primary language.
	problems with irregular subject-verb agreement *Sue and Ed has a new house.*	Cantonese, Hmong, Khmer, Korean, Tagalog	Verbs forms do not change to indicate the number of the subject in the primary language.
Past tense	omission of tense markers *I study English yesterday.* *I give it to him yesterday.*	Cantonese, Haitian Creole, Hmong, Khmer, Korean, Tagalog, Vietnamese	Verbs in the primary language do not change form to express tense.
	confusion of present form and simple past of irregular verbs *I give it to him yesterday.*	Cantonese, Spanish	Speakers of the primary language have difficulty recognizing that merely a vowel shift in the middle of the verb, rather than a change in the ending of the verb, is sufficient to produce a change of tense in irregular verbs.
	incorrect use of present for the future *I come tomorrow.*	Cantonese, Korean	The primary language allows the use of present tense for the future.
In negative statements	omission of helping verbs in negative statements *I no understand.* *I not get into university.*	Cantonese, Korean, Russian, Spanish, Tagalog	Helping verbs are not used in negative statements in the primary language.
Perfect tenses	avoidance of present perfect where it should be used *I live here for two years.*	Haitian Creole, Russian, Tagalog, Vietnamese	The verb form either doesn't exist in the primary language or has a different function.
	use of present perfect where past perfect should be used *Yesterday I have done that.*	Khmer, Korean	In the primary language a past marker, e.g., *yesterday*, is inserted to indicate a completed action and no other change is necessary. In English when a past marker is used, the verb form must change to past perfect instead of present perfect.
Past continuous	use of past continuous for recurring action in the past *When I was young, I was studying a lot.*	Korean, Spanish, Tagalog	In the primary language, the past continuous form can be used in contexts in which English uses the expression *used to* or the simple past.
Verb as a noun	omission of infinitive marker *to* *Criticize people is not good.*	Cantonese	Unlike English, Cantonese does not require an infinitive marker when using a verb as a noun.

Saxon Math

GRAMMAR POINT	TYPE OF TRANSFER ERROR IN ENGLISH	LANGUAGE BACKGROUND	CAUSE OF TRANSFER DIFFICULTY
	Use of two or more main verbs in one clause without any connectors *I took a book studied at the library.*	Hmong	In Hmong verbs can be connected without *and* or any other conjunction (serial verbs).
Linking verbs	Omission of linking verb *He hungry.*	Cantonese, Haitian Creole, Hmong, Khmer, Russian, Vietnamese	The verb *be* is not required in all sentences. In some primary languages, it is implied in the adjective form. In others the concept is expressed as a verb.
Passive voice	Omission of helping verb *be* in passive voice *The food finished.*	Cantonese, Vietnamese	Passive voice in the primary language does not require a helping verb.
	Avoidance of passive constructions *They speak Creole here.* *One speaks Creole here.* avoiding the alternate *Creole is spoken here.*	Haitian Creole	Passive constructions do not exist in Haitian Creole.
Transitive verbs versus intransitive verbs	confusion of transitive and intransitive verbs *He married with a nice girl.*	Cantonese, Korean, Russian, Spanish, Tagalog	Verbs that do and do not take a direct object differ between English and the primary language.
Phrasal verbs	confusion of related phrasal verbs *I look after the word in the dictionary.* instead of *I look up the word in the dictionary.*	Korean, Russian, Spanish	Phrasal verbs do not exist in the primary language. There is often confusion over their meaning in English.
have versus *be*	use of *have* instead of *be* *I have hunger.* *I have right.*	Spanish	Some Spanish constructions use *have* where English uses *be*.

Adverbs

GRAMMAR POINT	TYPE OF TRANSFER ERROR IN ENGLISH	LANGUAGE BACKGROUND	CAUSE OF TRANSFER DIFFICULTY
	use of adjective form where adverb form is needed *Walk quiet.*	Haitian Creole, Hmong, Khmer	There are no suffix-derived adverb forms in the primary language, and the adjective form is used after the verb.
	placement of adverbs before verbs *At ten o'clock this morning my plane landed.* avoiding the alternate, *My plane landed at ten o'clock this morning.*	Cantonese, Korean	Adverbs usually come before verbs in the primary language, and this tendency is carried over into English.

Prepositions

GRAMMAR POINT	TYPE OF TRANSFER ERROR IN ENGLISH	LANGUAGE BACKGROUND	CAUSE OF TRANSFER DIFFICULTY
	omission of prepositions *Money does not grow trees.*	Cantonese	There are no exact equivalents of English prepositions in Cantonese although there are words to mark location and movement.

Complex Sentences

GRAMMAR POINT	TYPE OF TRANSFER ERROR IN ENGLISH	LANGUAGE BACKGROUND	CAUSE OF TRANSFER DIFFICULTY
Relative clauses	omission of relative pronouns *My grandfather was a generous man helped everyone.*	Vietnamese	Relative pronouns are not required in Vietnamese.
	incorrect pronoun used to introduce a relative clause *the house <u>who</u> is big*	Hmong	Hmong uses the same forms of relative pronouns for both personal and inanimate antecedents.
Adverbial clauses	inclusion of additional connecting word *Because he was reckless, <u>so</u> he caused an accident.* *Although my parents are poor, <u>but</u> they are very generous.*	Cantonese, Korean, Vietnamese	The primary language sometimes uses a "balancing word" in the main clause.
	use of inconsistent tenses in sentences with multiple clauses *She <u>speaks</u> French before she <u>studied</u> English.* *After she <u>comes</u> home, it <u>was</u> <u>raining</u>.* *We <u>will go</u> to the beach if the weather <u>will be</u> nice.*	Cantonese, Hmong, Tagalog, Vietnamese	The primary language lacks tense markers so that matching the tenses of two verbs in one sentence correctly can be difficult. Learners may also try to analyze the tense needed in English according to meaning, which in some cases can result in the use of an incorrect tense.
If versus *when*	Confusion of *if* and *when* *If you get there, call me!* instead of *When you get there, call me!*	Korean, Tagalog	The primary language has one expression that covers the use of English *if* and *when* for the future.

Infinitives and Gerunds

GRAMMAR POINT	TYPE OF TRANSFER ERROR IN ENGLISH	LANGUAGE BACKGROUND	CAUSE OF TRANSFER DIFFICULTY
	use of present tense verbs in places where gerunds or infinitives are used in English *Stop walk.* *I want go there.*	Haitian Creole, Khmer, Korean	Either the *-ing* form does not exist in the primary language, or learners tend to use present tense verbs instead of gerunds even if they do exist [Haitian Creole].
	use of *for* in infinitive phrases *They went for to see the movie.*	Spanish	Spanish uses a prepositional form in similar constructions, which is carried over into English and translated as *for*.

Sentence Structure

GRAMMAR POINT	TYPE OF TRANSFER ERROR IN ENGLISH	LANGUAGE BACKGROUND	CAUSE OF TRANSFER DIFFICULTY
	omission of object *He dyed [his hair].* *Yes, I want [some].*	Korean	Korean tends to omit objects and noun phrases after verbs.
	lack of variety in the position of clauses *Because you weren't at home and I couldn't find you, I left.* avoiding the alternate, *I left because you weren't at home and I couldn't find you.*	Korean	Since main clauses always come last in Korean, there is a tendency to put the main clause last in English. This is not an error in English, but it leads to a lack of sentence variety.
	clauses that describe earlier actions come first *After I finish my homework, I will watch TV.* avoiding the alternate, *I will watch TV after I finish my homework.*	Cantonese, Korean	The pattern in the primary language is to describe what happens first while later occurrences follow. This is not an error in English, but it leads to a lack of sentence variety.
	placement of phrase with the indirect object before the direct object *They gave to the girl the book.*	Spanish	The phrase with the indirect object can come before the direct object in Spanish.
	placement of modifiers between verb and direct object *She speaks very well English.*	Korean, Spanish	Word order, including the placement of adverbials, is freer in the primary language than in English.
	use of double negatives *I no see nobody.*	Spanish	Spanish requires double negatives in many sentence structures.
	use of clauses for other structures *I want that you help me.*	Russian, Spanish	Verbs that take direct objects versus those that require clauses differ in the primary language and English.

Questions

GRAMMAR POINT	TYPE OF TRANSFER ERROR IN ENGLISH	LANGUAGE BACKGROUND	CAUSE OF TRANSFER DIFFICULTY
	avoidance of English inverted question forms in yes/no questions in favor of tag questions or intonation *You come tomorrow, OK?* *He goes to school with you?*	Cantonese, Haitian Creole, Khmer, Korean, Russian, Tagalog, Vietnamese	The primary language doesn't use subject-verb inversion in questions.
	lack of subject-verb inversion in questions with helping verbs *When she will be home?* *Where you are going?*	Cantonese, Hmong, Russian, Tagalog	In the primary language, word order is the same in some questions and statements, depending on the context.
	omission of *do* or *did* in questions *Where you went?*	Haitian Creole, Hmong, Khmer, Korean, Russian, Spanish, Tagalog	In the primary language, there is no exact counterpart to the *do/did* verb in questions.
Yes/no questions	incorrect answer form for yes/no questions A: *Do you want more food?* B: *I want.* A: *Do you have a pen?* B: *I not have.*	Cantonese, Hmong, Khmer, Korean, Russian	In the primary language, learners tend to answer yes by repeating the verb in the question. They tend to say no by using *not* and repeating the verb.
	positive answer to negative question A: *Aren't you going?* B: *Yes.* when the person is not going	Cantonese, Korean, Russian	The appropriate response pattern differs between the primary language and English.
Tag questions	incorrect tag questions *You want to go home, are you?*	Cantonese, Khmer, Korean, Vietnamese	The primary language has no exact counterpart to a tag question, forms them differently, or does not add *do/did* to questions.

Phonics Transfer Issues for Seven Languages

SOUND TRANSFER (PHONOLOGY)

The symbol ● identifies areas in which these primary language speakers may have some difficulty pronouncing and perceiving spoken English. The sound may not exist in the primary language, may exist but be pronounced somewhat differently, or may be confused with another sound. Sound production and perception issues impact phonics instruction.

Consonants

SOUND	SPANISH	VIETNAMESE	HMONG	CANTONESE	HAITIAN CREOLE	KOREAN	KHMER
/b/ as in bat			●	●		●	
/k/ as in cat and kite			●				
/d/ as in dog				●		●	
/f/ as in fan						●	
/g/ as in goat			●	●		●	●
/h/ as in hen					●		
/j/ as in jacket	●	●	●	●		●	
/l/ as in lemon						●	
/m/ as in money							
/n/ as in nail							
/p/ as in pig			●				
/r/ as in rabbit	●		●	●	●	●	
/s/ as in sun			●				
/t/ as in teen		●	●				
/v/ as in video	●			●		●	●
/w/ as in wagon	●		●				●
/y/ as in yo-yo							
/z/ as in zebra	●		●	●		●	●
/kw/ as in queen			●				
/ks/ as in Xray			●	●			

Short Vowels

SOUND	SPANISH	VIETNAMESE	HMONG	CANTONESE	HAITIAN CREOLE	KOREAN	KHMER
short a as in hat	●	●		●		●	
short e as in set	●		●	●	●	●	
short i as in sit	●	●	●	●	●	●	
short o as in hot	●		●			●	
short u as in cup	●		●	●	●	●	

Long Vowels

SOUND	SPANISH	VIETNAMESE	HMONG	CANTONESE	HAITIAN CREOLE	KOREAN	KHMER
long *a* as in d<u>a</u>te			•	•			
long *e* as in b<u>e</u>				•		•	
long *i* as in <u>i</u>ce				•			
long *o* as in r<u>oa</u>d			•	•			
long *u* as in tr<u>ue</u>				•		•	

Vowel Patterns

SOUND	SPANISH	VIETNAMESE	HMONG	CANTONESE	HAITIAN CREOLE	KOREAN	KHMER
oo as in b<u>oo</u>k	•	•	•		•	•	•
aw as in s<u>aw</u>	•					•	

Diphthongs

SOUND	SPANISH	VIETNAMESE	HMONG	CANTONESE	HAITIAN CREOLE	KOREAN	KHMER
oy as in b<u>oy</u>			•				
ow as in h<u>ow</u>	•						

R-controlled Vowels

SOUND	SPANISH	VIETNAMESE	HMONG	CANTONESE	HAITIAN CREOLE	KOREAN	KHMER
ir as in b<u>ir</u>d	•	•	•	•	•	•	•
ar as in h<u>ar</u>d	•	•	•	•	•	•	•
or as in f<u>or</u>m	•	•	•	•	•	•	•
air as in h<u>air</u>	•	•	•	•	•	•	•
ear as in h<u>ear</u>	•	•	•	•	•	•	•

Consonant Digraphs

SOUND	SPANISH	VIETNAMESE	HMONG	CANTONESE	HAITIAN CREOLE	KOREAN	KHMER
sh as in <u>sh</u>oe *	•	•		•			•
ch as in <u>ch</u>ain		•		•			
th as in <u>th</u>ink	•	•	•	•		•	•
ng as in si<u>ng</u>	•		•		•		

Consonant Blends

SOUND	SPANISH	VIETNAMESE	HMONG	CANTONESE	HAITIAN CREOLE	KOREAN	KHMER
bl, *tr*, *dr*, etc. (start of words) as in <u>bl</u>ack, <u>tr</u>ee, <u>dr</u>ess		•	•	•		•	
ld, *nt*, *rt*, etc. (end of words) as in co<u>ld</u>, te<u>nt</u>, sta<u>rt</u>		•	•	•	•	•	•

*Spanish speakers from Mexico or Central America who also speak Nahuatl or a Mayan language will be familiar with this sound, written as an *x* in words like *mixteca* (pronounced *mishteca*).

SOUND-SYMBOL TRANSFER (PHONICS)

The following chart identifies sound-symbol transfer issues for four languages that use the Roman alphabet (the remaining three do not). The symbol ● identifies symbols which do not represent the corresponding sound in the writing system of the primary language.

Consonants

SOUND-SYMBOLS	SPANISH	VIETNAMESE	HMONG	HAITIAN CREOLE
b as in <u>b</u>at			●	
c as in <u>c</u>at		●	●	●
as in <u>c</u>ent		●	●	
d as in <u>d</u>og				
f as in <u>f</u>ish				
g as in <u>g</u>oat			●	
as in <u>g</u>iant	●		●	
h as in <u>h</u>en	●			
j as in <u>j</u>acket	●	●	●	
k as in <u>k</u>ite			●	
l as in <u>l</u>emon				
m as in <u>m</u>oon				
n as in <u>n</u>ice				
p as in <u>p</u>ig				
qu as in <u>qu</u>een	●		●	●
r as in <u>r</u>abbit	●		●	
s as in <u>s</u>un			●	
t as in <u>t</u>een			●	
v as in <u>v</u>ideo	●			
w as in <u>w</u>agon		●	●	
x as in <u>X</u>ray		●	●	●
y as in <u>y</u>o-<u>y</u>o	●			
z as in <u>z</u>ebra	●	●	●	

Consonant Digraphs

SOUND-SYMBOLS	SPANISH	VIETNAMESE	HMONG	HAITIAN CREOLE
sh as in <u>sh</u>oe	●			
ch as in <u>ch</u>air				●
th as in <u>th</u>ink	●			●
as in <u>th</u>at				

Vowels and Vowel Patterns

SOUND-SYMBOLS	SPANISH	VIETNAMESE	HMONG	HAITIAN CREOLE
a as in b<u>a</u>t	●		●	
aCe as in d<u>a</u>te	●	●		
ai as in r<u>ai</u>n	●	●	●	●
ay as in d<u>ay</u>	●		●	●
au as in <u>au</u>thor	●	●	●	●
aw as in s<u>aw</u>	●	●	●	●
e as in b<u>e</u>t	●		●	●
ee as in s<u>ee</u>d	●	●	●	●
ea as in t<u>ea</u>	●	●	●	●
ew as in f<u>ew</u>	●	●	●	●
i as in s<u>i</u>t	●		●	●
iCe as in p<u>i</u>pe	●	●	●	●
o as in h<u>o</u>t	●		●	●
o as in r<u>o</u>de	●	●	●	●
oo as in m<u>oo</u>n	●	●	●	●
oo as in b<u>oo</u>k	●		●	●
oa as in b<u>oa</u>t	●	●	●	●
ow as in r<u>ow</u>	●	●		●
ow as in h<u>ow</u>	●	●	●	●
ou as in s<u>ou</u>nd	●	●	●	●
oi as in b<u>oi</u>l			●	●
oy as in b<u>oy</u>		●	●	●
u as in c<u>u</u>p	●	●	●	●
uCe as in J<u>u</u>ne	●	●		
ui as in s<u>ui</u>t	●	●	●	●
ue as in bl<u>ue</u>	●	●	●	●
y as in tr<u>y</u>	●	●	●	●
ar as in st<u>ar</u>			●	●
er as in f<u>er</u>n	●		●	●
ir as in b<u>ir</u>d	●		●	●
or as in t<u>or</u>n	●		●	
ur as in b<u>ur</u>n	●		●	